ATLAS OF MEDIEVAL BRITAIN

Christopher Daniell's *Atlas of Medieval Britain* presents a sweeping visual survey of Britain from the Roman occupation to 1485.

Annotated throughout with clear commentary, this volume tells the story of the British Isles, and makes visually accessible the varied and often complex world of the Middle Ages. The atlas depicts the spatial distribution of key events and buildings between 1066 and 1485, as well as providing the relevant Anglo-Saxon background. Charting the main political, administrative and religious features of medieval society, the maps also locate cultural landmarks such as the sites of Mystery Plays, universities and specific architectural styles.

Topics covered include:

- Iron Age and Roman occupation
- Anglo-Saxons and Vikings
- Changing political scenarios within England, Scotland, Wales and Ireland
- Religious framework, including diocesan boundaries, monasteries and friaries
- Government, society and economy.

Complete with recommended further reading, this volume is an indispensable reference resource for all students of medieval British history.

Christopher Daniell is a Research Associate and former Honorary Visiting Fellow at the Centre for Medieval Studies, University of York. He is the author of *From Norman Conquest to Magna Carta, England 1066–1215* (Routledge, 2003). He currently works as Historic Building Advisor for the Government.

ATLAS
of
MEDIEVAL BRITAIN

CHRISTOPHER DANIELL

Routledge
Taylor & Francis Group

LONDON AND NEW YORK

First published 2008
First published in paperback 2011
by Routledge
2 Park Square, Milton Park, Abingdon, Oxon OX14 4RN

Simultaneously published in the USA and Canada
by Routledge
270 Madison Avenue, New York, NY 10016

Routledge is an imprint of the Taylor & Francis Group, an informa business

© 2008, 2011 Christopher Daniell

Typeset in Garamond by RefineCatch Limited, Bungay, Suffolk
Printed and bound in Great Britain by
MPG Books Ltd, Bodmin

British Library Cataloguing in Publication Data
A catalogue record for this book is available from the British Library

Library of Congress Cataloging in Publication Data
Daniell, Christopher.
    Atlas of medieval Britain / Christopher Daniell.
        p. cm.
    Includes bibliographical references and index.
    1. Great Britain–History–Medieval period, 1066–1485–Maps.
2. Great Britain–Politics and government–1066–1485–Maps.
3. Great Britain–Civilization–1066–1485–Maps.   4. Great
Britain–Social life and customs–1066–1485–Maps.   I. Title.
G1812.21.S1D3 2008
911'.41–dc22
                                                    2007050655

ISBN: 978–0–415–34069–4 (hbk)
ISBN: 978–0–415–60223–5 (pbk)

CONTENTS

RELIGION AND CULTURE

PREFACE AND ACKNOWLEDGEMENTS

This atlas primarily covers the period 1066–1500 for England, Scotland, Wales and Ireland. It attempts to represent the huge diversity of evidence that exists from this period, whether economic, religious, political or cultural. These divisions follow the magnificent companion volume to this one, the *Atlas of Medieval Europe,* edited by David Ditchburn, Simon Maclean and Angus Mackay, which is also published by Routledge.

The period saw the British Isles undergo major changes, whether through the Norman Conquest of England, Wales, and later Ireland, or the rise of the power of Scotland as a nation. Further wars and invasions followed thereafter, such as the Hundred Years War or The Wars of the Roses. Not only are the shifting politics represented in the maps, but also the social tensions – whether Black Death or Peasant's Revolt – and cultural aspects, such as the Mystery Plays or the development of architecture.

Some introductory maps have been included to put the later maps into context. However, as the Anglo-Saxon period (500–1066) has previously been covered in great detail by David Hill's *An Atlas of Anglo-Saxon England* it has not been thought necessary to simply replicate them in this Atlas. Similarly I have concentrated solely on the British Isles, as Europe has been covered in the *Atlas of Medieval Europe.*

Some maps I have drawn – to my knowledge – for the first time (for example, the regional impact of certain markets or fairs), whilst other maps necessarily follow other authorities, though with my own interpretation. I hope that the maps will provide a useful starting point for future exploration, and explanation, of the fascinating period between 1066 and 1500.

Accuracy is an important part of any map and my aim was to be as accurate as possible, though in some cases intelligent guesswork had to be employed where sites are lost or information is hazy or disputed. However, I have not set 'traps' for the unwary by deliberately mis-placing or misspelling locations – this does mean, however, that I am solely responsible for any mistakes that have occurred. If errors have occurred I would be grateful to know. Equally I have attempted to be as clear as possible, though there is always a balance to be struck between clarity and more or less data. Time and the reader will tell if I have succeeded.

Finally I would like to acknowledge Cambridge University Press and Shire Books for their permissions to use some of their maps (redrawn by the author) and to Fr Richard Copsey for generously sharing his data on the Carmelite distinctions. I would also like to thank my editors, originally Victoria Peters and, more recently, Eve Setch and Elizabeth Clifford. Finally I would like to thank my wife Alison, who has had to put up with me working long evenings in order to create and produce the maps in this book.

Christopher Daniell

MAPS

1. Physical Geography of the British Isles

Orkney Islands

Shetland Islands

Outer Hebrides

North West Highlands

Grampians

SCOTLAND

Southern Uplands

ATLANTIC OCEAN

NORTH SEA

R. Tyne

R. Tees

North York Moors

Cumbrian Mts

Yorkshire Wolds

Northern Ireland

Lough Neagh

Isle of Man

IRELAND

Pennines

IRISH SEA

R. Shannon

ENGLAND

R. Trent

Fens

Norfolk Broads

Cambrian Mts

R. Severn

WALES

Chiltern Hills

Cotswolds

R. Thames

Brecon Beacons

Exmoor

Dartmoor

Salisbury Plain

Weald

Isle of Wight

ENGLISH CHANNEL

Land over 1000m (3000 ft)

Major river

C. Daniell

3

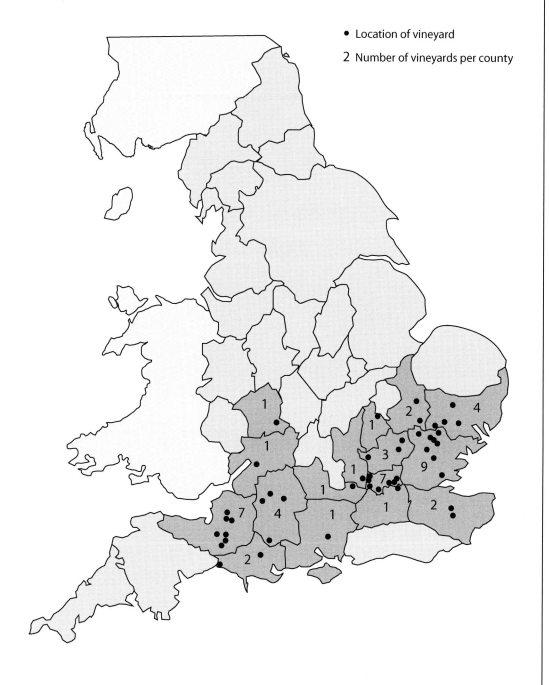

2. Vineyards in the 1086 Domesday Book

• Location of vineyard

2 Number of vineyards per county

The location and number of vineyards recorded in the Domesday Book of 1086 shows that the climate was warmer than at present. There were also probably vineyards elsewhere, such as in Sussex and Devon.

C. Daniell

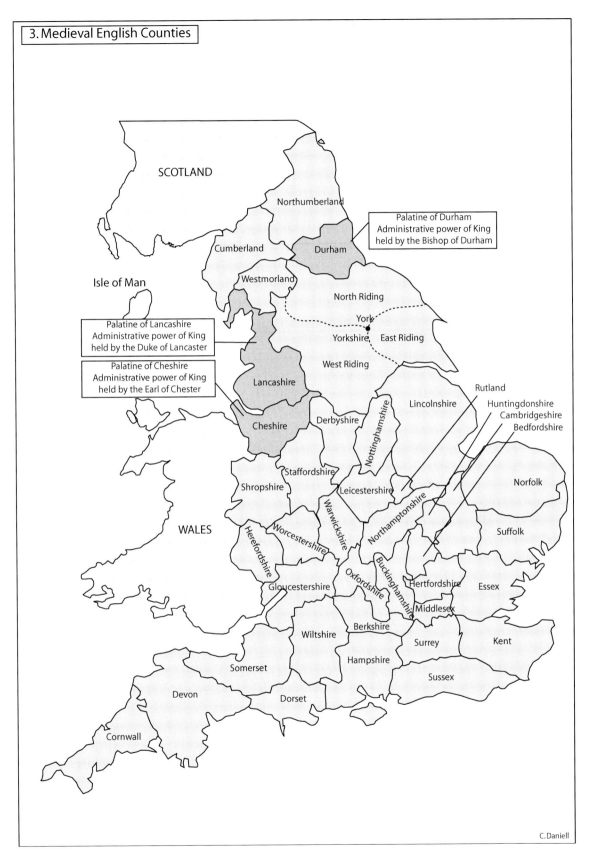

3. Medieval English Counties

SCOTLAND

Northumberland

Cumberland

Durham

Palatine of Durham
Administrative power of King
held by the Bishop of Durham

Westmorland

North Riding

Isle of Man

York

Yorkshire   East Riding

Palatine of Lancashire
Administrative power of King
held by the Duke of Lancaster

West Riding

Palatine of Cheshire
Administrative power of King
held by the Earl of Chester

Lancashire

Lincolnshire

Rutland

Huntingdonshire
Cambridgeshire
Bedfordshire

Cheshire

Derbyshire

Nottinghamshire

Staffordshire

Norfolk

Shropshire

Leicestershire

WALES

Warwickshire

Northamptonshire

Suffolk

Herefordshire

Worcestershire

Oxfordshire

Buckinghamshire

Hertfordshire

Essex

Gloucestershire

Middlesex

Berkshire

Wiltshire

Surrey

Kent

Hampshire

Somerset

Sussex

Devon

Dorset

Cornwall

C. Daniell

5

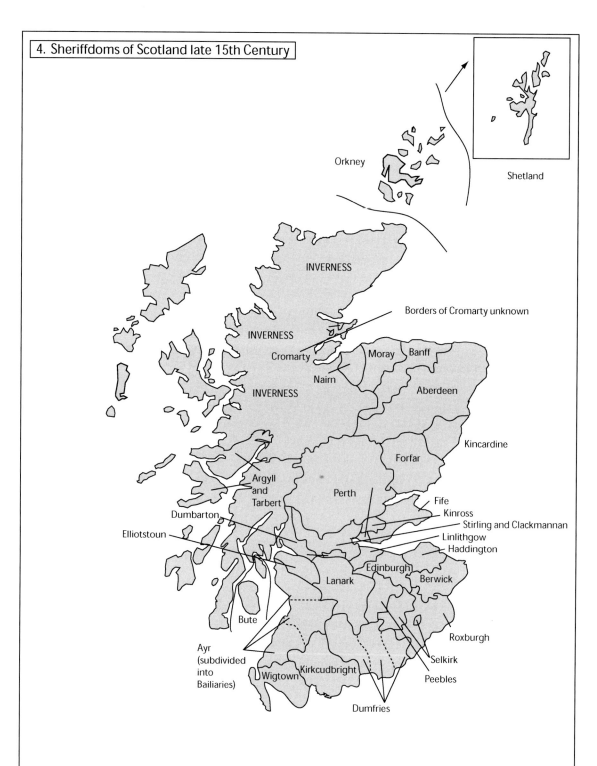

4. Sheriffdoms of Scotland late 15th Century

Shetland

Orkney

INVERNESS

INVERNESS

Borders of Cromarty unknown

Cromarty

Moray   Banff

Nairn

Aberdeen

INVERNESS

Kincardine

Forfar

Argyll
and
Tarbert

Perth

Fife

Kinross

Dumbarton

Stirling and Clackmannan

Elliotstoun

Linlithgow

Haddington

Edinburgh

Lanark

Berwick

Bute

Roxburgh

Ayr
(subdivided
into
Bailiaries)

Selkirk

Wigtown   Kirkcudbright

Peebles

Dumfries

Sheriffdoms developed out of earlier units of mormaerdoms, bailiaries, sheriffdoms and stewartries. Some areas were sub-divided (such as the Bailiaries of Ayrshire). The sheriffs of the regions were powerful nobles could influence the crown and played an important role in the politics of Scotland.

C. Daniell

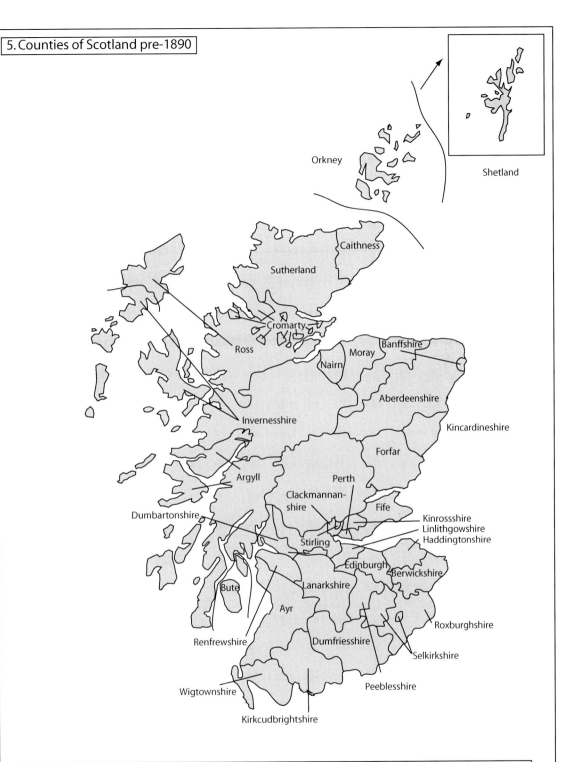

5. Counties of Scotland pre-1890

Shetland

Orkney

Shetland

Caithness

Sutherland

Cromarty

Ross

Banffshire

Moray

Nairn

Aberdeenshire

Invernesshire

Kincardineshire

Forfar

Argyll

Perth

Clackmannan-
shire

Fife

Kinrossshire
Linlithgowshire
Haddingtonshire

Dumbartonshire

Stirling

Edinburgh

Berwickshire

Bute

Lanarkshire

Ayr

Roxburghshire

Renfrewshire

Dumfriesshire

Selkirkshire

Wigtownshire

Peeblesshire

Kirkcudbrightshire

The counties of Scotland evolved out of earlier administrative boundaries, in particular sheriffdoms. Before 19th-century reorganisation many counties had enclaves of other counties within them, in particular Ross, which contained fragments of Cromarty. Cromarty's borders were finally stabilised in the late 17th century.

C. Daniell

7

6. Welsh Historic Counties

Anglesey* (Sir Fon)

Caernarfonshire* (Sir Gaernarfon)

Flintshire (Sir y Fflint)

Denbighshire** (Sir Ddinbych)

Cheshire

Merioneth* (Sir Feirionnydd / Meirionydd)

Shropshire

E N G L A N D

Montgomeryshire** (Sir Drefaldwyn)

Radnorshire** (Sir Faesyfed)

Cardiganshire* (Ceredigion / Sir Aberteifi)

Herefordshire

Pembrokeshire (Sir Benfro)

Carmarthenshire* (Sir Gaerfyrddin / Sir Gar)

Brecknockshire** (Sir Frycheiniog)

Glamorgan (Morgannwyg / Sir Forgannwg)

Monmouthshire (Sir Fynwy)

Monmouthshire – English county names

(Sir Fynwy) – Welsh county names

* Counties orginated in 1282 after Edward I's conquest

** Marcher Lordships converted into counties in 1535

The historic counties were often based on older divisions of Wales, such as an earldom (Pembroke) or lordships (Glamorgan, Marcher lordships). Monmouthshire was also created in 1535, but was legally part of England until 1974.

C. Daniell

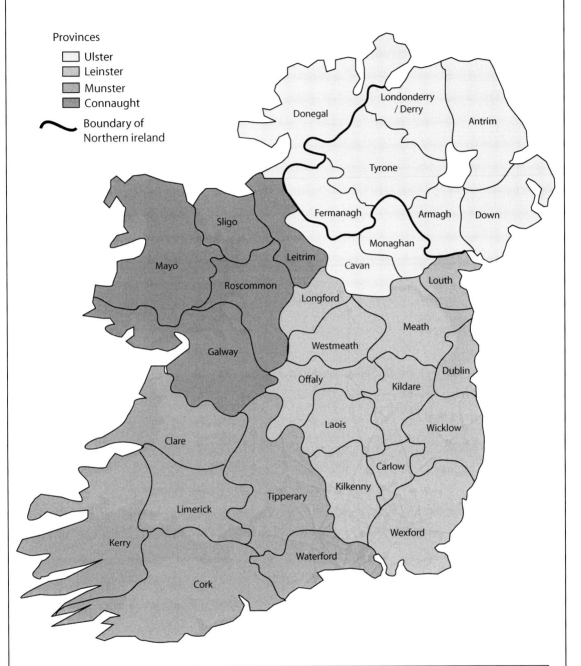

7. Irish Historic Provinces and Counties

Provinces

- Ulster
- Leinster
- Munster
- Connaught
- ～ Boundary of Northern ireland

Donegal

Londonderry / Derry

Antrim

Tyrone

Fermanagh

Armagh

Down

Monaghan

Cavan

Sligo

Leitrim

Louth

Mayo

Roscommon

Longford

Meath

Galway

Westmeath

Dublin

Offaly

Kildare

Laois

Wicklow

Clare

Carlow

Kilkenny

Tipperary

Limerick

Wexford

Kerry

Waterford

Cork

Whilst there are the traditional 32 counties of Ireland (26 in the Republic, 6 in Northern Ireland) the process of formation took many centuries. The earliest were generally in the English-controlled areas where the county system was often imposed on older boundaries. Counties were carved out of the four older provinces and the division of Connaught occurred in the late 16th century. The last county to be created was Wicklow in 1606, a combination of lands from County Dublin and Carlow.

C. Daniell

ROMAN AND EARLY MIDDLE AGES

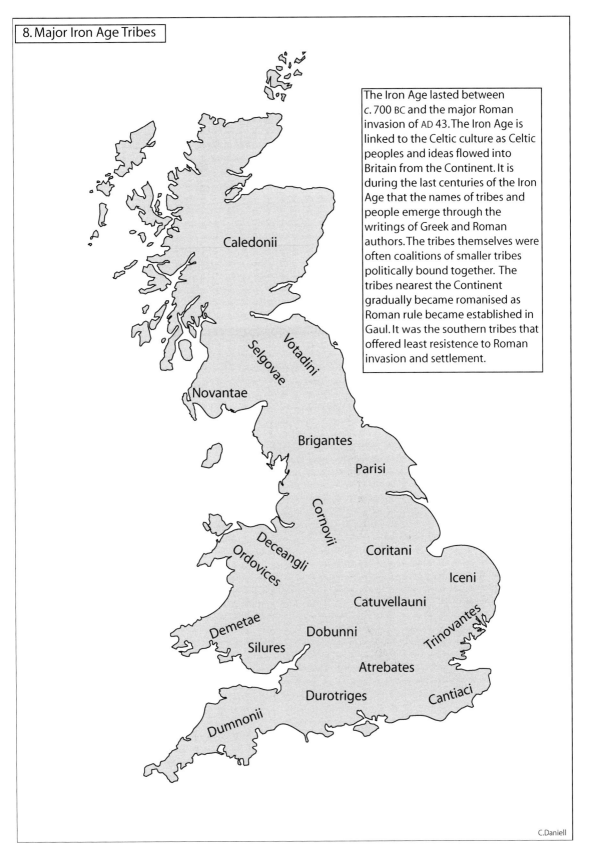

8. Major Iron Age Tribes

The Iron Age lasted between *c*. 700 BC and the major Roman invasion of AD 43. The Iron Age is linked to the Celtic culture as Celtic peoples and ideas flowed into Britain from the Continent. It is during the last centuries of the Iron Age that the names of tribes and people emerge through the writings of Greek and Roman authors. The tribes themselves were often coalitions of smaller tribes politically bound together. The tribes nearest the Continent gradually became romanised as Roman rule became established in Gaul. It was the southern tribes that offered least resistence to Roman invasion and settlement.

Caledonii

Votadini

Selgovae

Novantae

Brigantes

Parisi

Cornovii

Deceangli

Ordovices

Coritani

Iceni

Catuvellauni

Demetae

Dobunni

Trinovantes

Silures

Atrebates

Durotriges

Cantiaci

Dumnonii

C.Daniell

13

9. Roman Province of Britannia AD 212–296

Britannia Superior — Name of province

● Provincial capital

□ Legionary fortress

Picts

Independent British tribes

Antonine Wall – started AD 142 and in use until AD 164, and briefly after AD 208.

Hadrian's Wall – started AD 122. Formed the northern boundary before and after Antonine Wall in use.

Britannia Inferior

York ●□

Chester □

Caerleon □

Britannia Superior

London ●

The Romans invaded Britain three times, twice by Julius Caesar, in 55 BC and then the next year, 54 BC. These were brief campaigns. The large-scale invasion took place in AD 43. Initially 'Britannia' was treated as a single entity but Caracalla split the province into two in AD 212. Britannia Superior was governed from London with two legionary fortresses, one at Chester and the other at Caerleon. Although early campaigns marched into Scotland, the northern boundary was later demarcated by Hadrian's Wall.

C. Daniell

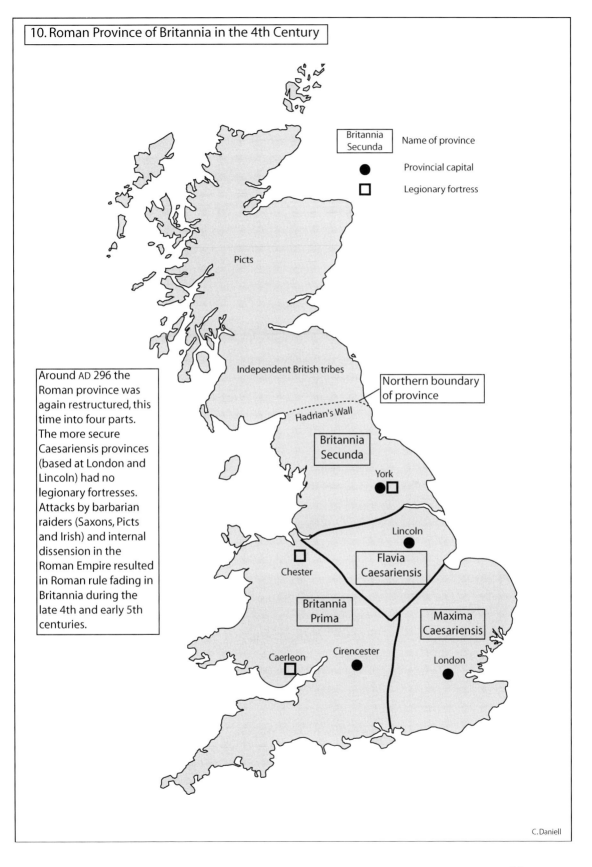

10. Roman Province of Britannia in the 4th Century

Britannia Secunda — Name of province

● Provincial capital

□ Legionary fortress

Picts

Independent British tribes

Northern boundary of province

Hadrian's Wall

Britannia Secunda

York

Lincoln

Flavia Caesariensis

Chester

Britannia Prima

Maxima Caesariensis

Caerleon

Cirencester

London

Around AD 296 the Roman province was again restructured, this time into four parts. The more secure Caesariensis provinces (based at London and Lincoln) had no legionary fortresses. Attacks by barbarian raiders (Saxons, Picts and Irish) and internal dissension in the Roman Empire resulted in Roman rule fading in Britannia during the late 4th and early 5th centuries.

C. Daniell

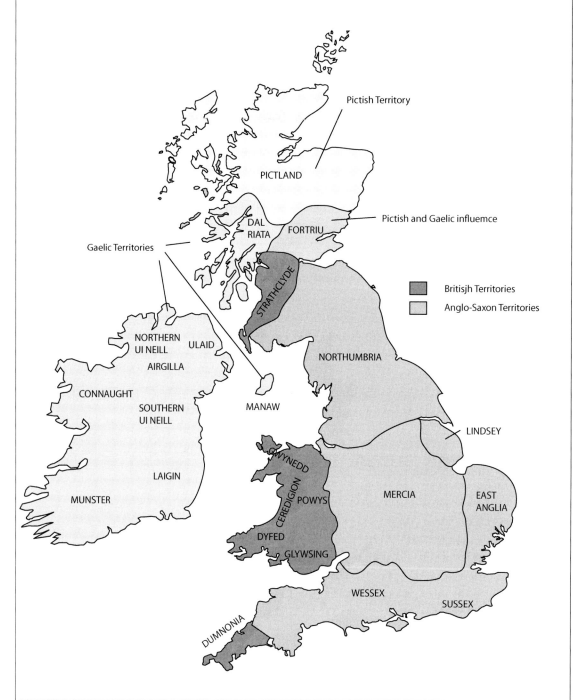

11. Kingdoms in the British Isles *c.* AD 800

Pictish Territory

PICTLAND

Pictish and Gaelic influemce

DAL
RIATA   FORTRIU

Gaelic Territories

STRATHCLYDE

Britisjh Territories

Anglo-Saxon Territories

NORTHERN
UI NEILL   ULAID

AIRGILLA

NORTHUMBRIA

CONNAUGHT

SOUTHERN
UI NEILL

MANAW

LINDSEY

LAIGIN

GWYNEDD

MUNSTER

CEREDIGION   POWYS

MERCIA

EAST
ANGLIA

DYFED

GLYWSING

WESSEX

SUSSEX

DUMNONIA

From *c.* AD 450 onwards the Anglo-Saxons from Saxony and Denmark invaded England. By *c.* 800 Anglo-Saxon kingdoms had formed across England and the native British had been pushed westwards by the Anglo-Saxon invasions. In Ireland and Scotland there were either Gaelic or Pictish territories.

C. Daniell

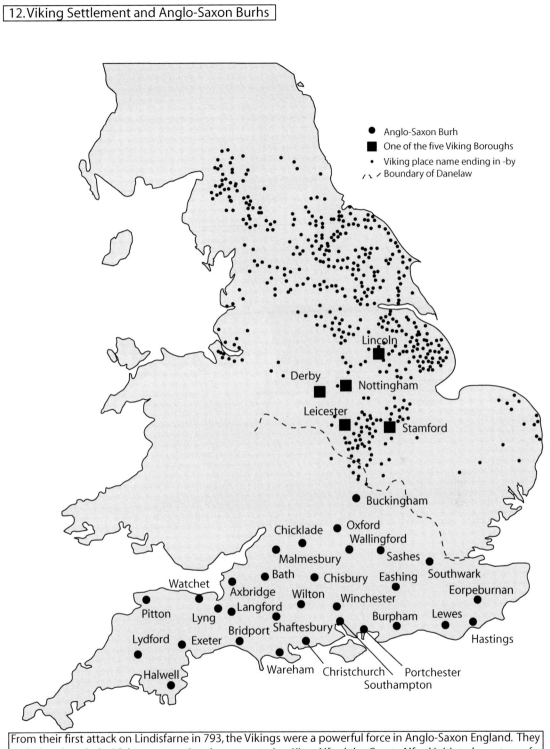

12. Viking Settlement and Anglo-Saxon Burhs

● Anglo-Saxon Burh
■ One of the five Viking Boroughs
· Viking place name ending in -by
⌐ ̫ ̣ Boundary of Danelaw

Lincoln

Derby

Nottingham

Leicester

Stamford

Buckingham

Chicklade

Oxford

Wallingford

Malmesbury

Sashes

Bath

Chisbury

Eashing

Southwark

Watchet

Axbridge

Wilton

Winchester

Eorpeburnan

Pitton

Langford

Lyng

Burpham

Lewes

Lydford

Bridport

Shaftesbury

Exeter

Hastings

Halwell

Wareham

Christchurch

Portchester

Southampton

From their first attack on Lindisfarne in 793, the Vikings were a powerful force in Anglo-Saxon England. They raided and settled widely, at one point almost capturing King Alfred the Great. Alfred initiated a system of fortified settlements, burhs, as a defence against the fast-moving Vikings. Eventually a truce was agreed, but the wars soon resumed. After a long period of success by the Wessex kings, the Viking Cnut eventually conquered the country.

C. Daniell

13. Anglo-Saxon Dioceses in 9th Century

Borders of diocese unknown

Area of disruption to dioceses caused by Viking attacks c. 900

Caistor ▙ Location of Cathedral

Lindisfarne ▙

Hexham ▙

In 735 York became the second archdiocese, with oversight of the northern dioceses.

York ▙

Caistor ▙

Lichfield ▙

Leicester ▙

Elmham ▙

Hereford ▙

Worcester ▙

Dunwich ▙

Dorchester ▙

London ▙

Rochester ▙

Winchester ▙

Sherborne ▙

Selsey ▙

Canterbury

Canterbury was the first archdiocese and had oversight of all dioceses until the creation of the Archdiocese of York.

The set pattern of dioceses in the mid-9th century was seriously disrupted by Viking invasions. The disruption either resulted in dioceses merging, such as Dunwich with Elmham, or the centre of the diocese moving, as in the case of Leicester to Dorchester. King Athelstan of Wessex continued his ancestor's conquests and reunited England under one king, thereby allowing the church to recover in the disrupted areas.

C. Daniell

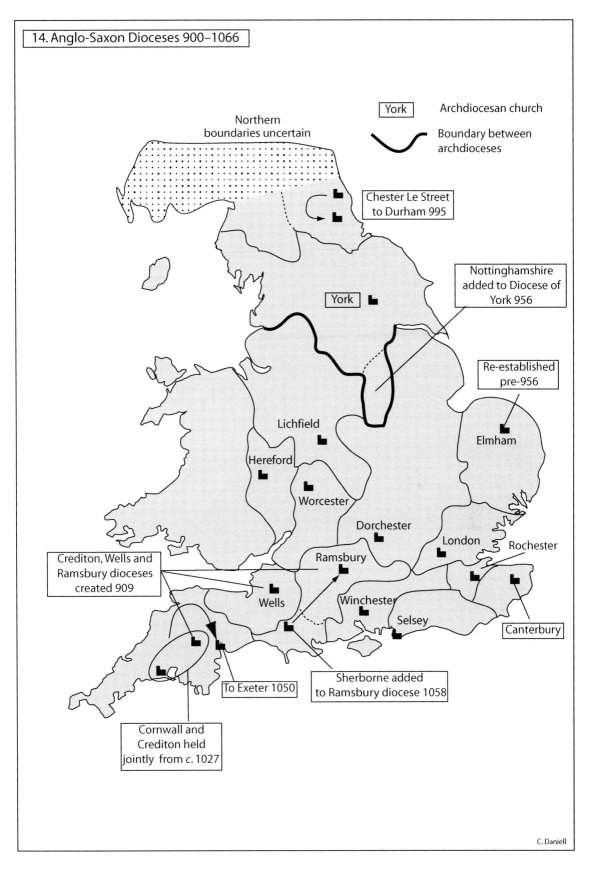

14. Anglo-Saxon Dioceses 900–1066

York — Archdiocesan church

Boundary between archdioceses

Northern boundaries uncertain

Chester Le Street to Durham 995

York

Nottinghamshire added to Diocese of York 956

Re-established pre-956

Elmham

Lichfield

Hereford

Worcester

Dorchester

London

Rochester

Crediton, Wells and Ramsbury dioceses created 909

Ramsbury

Wells

Winchester

Selsey

Canterbury

To Exeter 1050

Sherborne added to Ramsbury diocese 1058

Cornwall and Crediton held jointly from c. 1027

C. Daniell

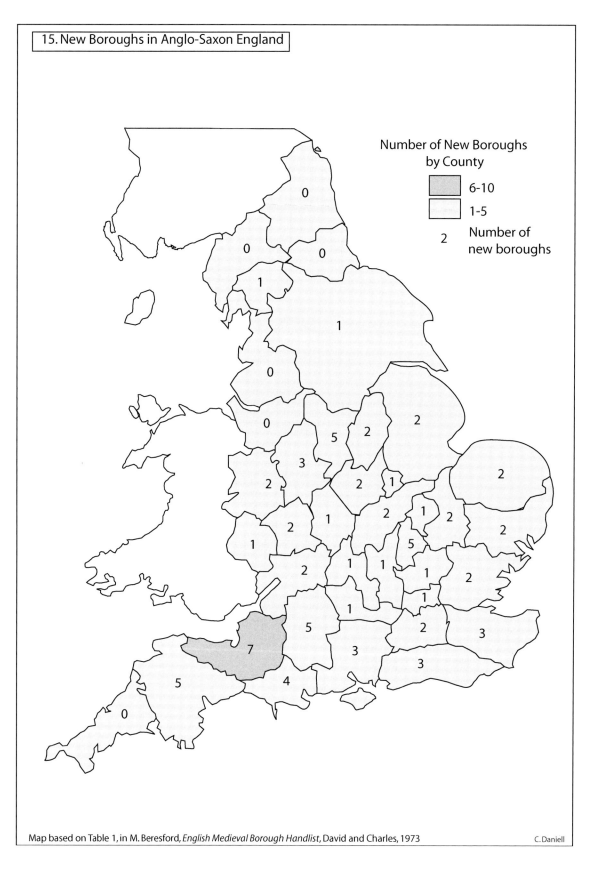

15. New Boroughs in Anglo-Saxon England

Number of New Boroughs
by County

6-10

1-5

2   Number of
     new boroughs

Map based on Table 1, in M. Beresford, *English Medieval Borough Handlist*, David and Charles, 1973

C. Daniell

16. Mints of Edward the Confessor

York

Buckingham
Wallingford
Bedford
Huntingdon
Cambridge

Lincoln

Chester

Derby

Nottingham

Stamford

Norwich

Stafford

Tamworth

Leicester

Thetford

Shrewsbury

Bury St Edmunds
Ipswich

Worcester

Warwick

Northampton

Sudbury

Pershore

Hereford

Winchcombe

Gloucester

Oxford

Hertford

Colchester

Berkeley

Cricklade

Reading

Horndon

Bristol
Frome

Malmesbury

Bedwyn

Rochester
Canterbury

Sandwich

Watchet

Guildford

Dover

Barnstaple

Taunton

Winchester

Lewes

Hythe
Romney

Lydford

Chichester

Hastings

Exeter

Bridport

Salisbury

London

Wilton

Southwark

Warminster

Wareham

Shaftesbury

Dorcester

Bristol
Bath
Frome
Watchet
Langport
Taunton
Ilchester

Petherton

Data based on information in Corpus of Early Medieval Coin Finds and Sylloge of Coins of the British Isles

C. Daniell

21

17. Wales in the Mid-11th Century

Chester

Atiscross

R. Clwyd

Exestan

Dudestan

Mersete

GWYNEDD

6

ARDUDWY

MEIRIONYDD

Oswestry
Shrewsbury

POWYS

Montgomery

1

RHWNG
GWY
A
HAFREN

Radnor

E
N
G
L
A
N
D

CEREDIGION

Hereford

3

BRYCHEINIOG

EWIAS

DYFED

DEHEUBARTH

Archen
field

Monmouth

2

5

Caerleon

4

GLAMORGAN

1 1039–1044 Gruffydd ap Llywelyn
of Gwynedd captures west Wales
2 1049–1055 Gruffydd ravages and
captures south Wales
3 1055 Gruffydd and Norse allies
sack Hereford
4 1049 English defeated at
Tidenham
5 1063 King Harold of England
attacks. South Wales submits to him
6 1063 Gruffydd murdered

Fought-over areas

Atiscross   Welsh advance into
English hundreds

▬ ▬ ▬ Offa's Dyke

Areas of border
raids by Welsh

C. Daniell

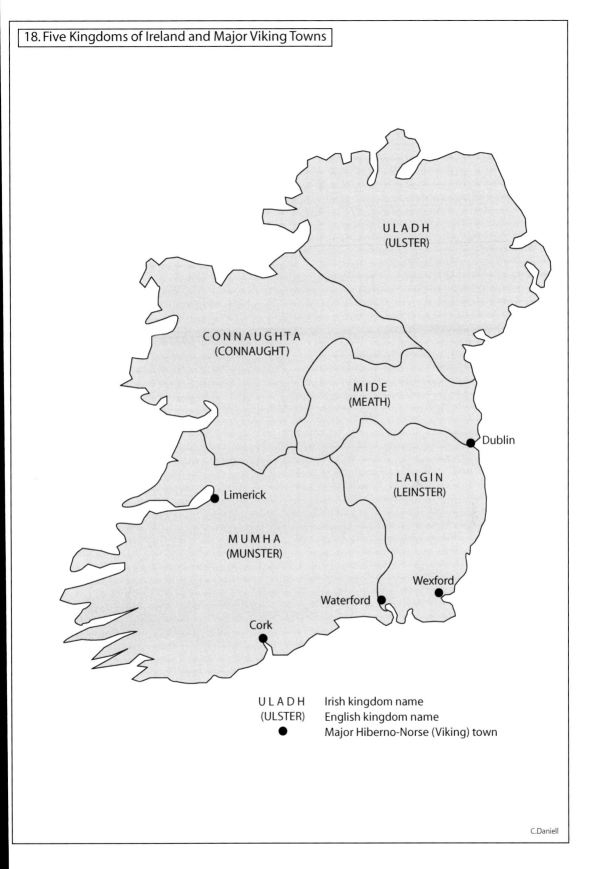

ULADH
(ULSTER)

CONNAUGHTA
(CONNAUGHT)

MIDE
(MEATH)

● Dublin

LAIGIN
(LEINSTER)

● Limerick

MUMHA
(MUNSTER)

Wexford ●

Waterford ●

Cork
●

ULADH   Irish kingdom name
(ULSTER)   English kingdom name
●   Major Hiberno-Norse (Viking) town

C.Daniell

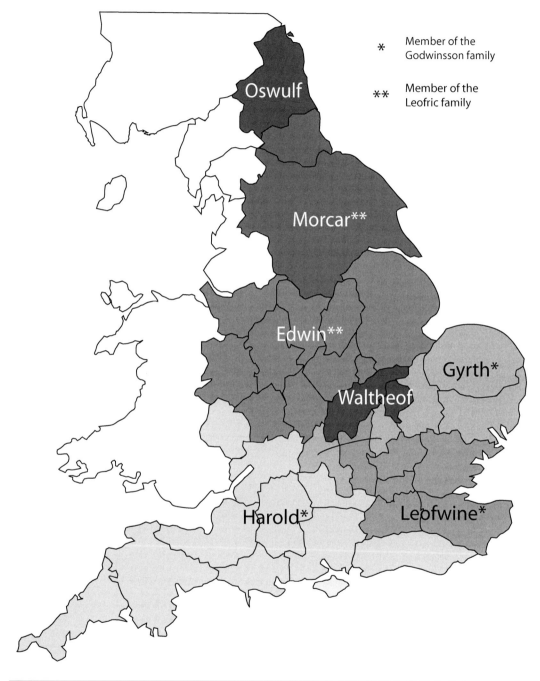

* Member of the Godwinsson family

** Member of the Leofric family

Oswulf

Morcar**

Edwin**

Gyrth*

Waltheof

Harold*

Leofwine*

The Anglo-Saxon earls were second only in power to the King, Edward the Confessor. The earldoms were mainly divided between the Godwinsson and the Leofric families. When Edward the Confessor died in 1066, Earl Harold seized the throne and was defeated later in the same year by Duke William of Normandy.

C. Daniell

CENTRAL AND LATE MEDIEVAL PERIOD

WAR AND POLITICS

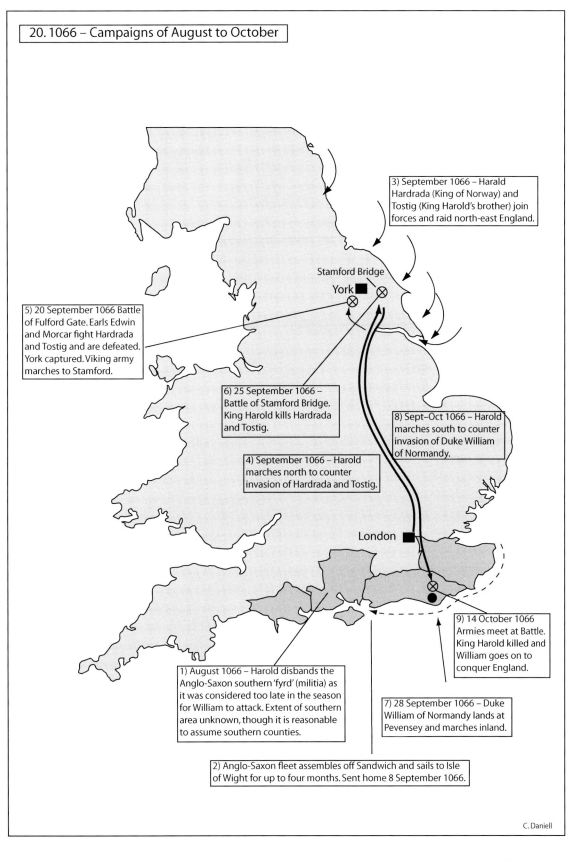

20. 1066 – Campaigns of August to October

3) September 1066 – Harald Hardrada (King of Norway) and Tostig (King Harold's brother) join forces and raid north-east England.

5) 20 September 1066 Battle of Fulford Gate. Earls Edwin and Morcar fight Hardrada and Tostig and are defeated. York captured. Viking army marches to Stamford.

Stamford Bridge

York

6) 25 September 1066 – Battle of Stamford Bridge. King Harold kills Hardrada and Tostig.

8) Sept–Oct 1066 – Harold marches south to counter invasion of Duke William of Normandy.

4) September 1066 – Harold marches north to counter invasion of Hardrada and Tostig.

London

9) 14 October 1066 Armies meet at Battle. King Harold killed and William goes on to conquer England.

1) August 1066 – Harold disbands the Anglo-Saxon southern 'fyrd' (militia) as it was considered too late in the season for William to attack. Extent of southern area unknown, though it is reasonable to assume southern counties.

7) 28 September 1066 – Duke William of Normandy lands at Pevensey and marches inland.

2) Anglo-Saxon fleet assembles off Sandwich and sails to Isle of Wight for up to four months. Sent home 8 September 1066.

C. Daniell

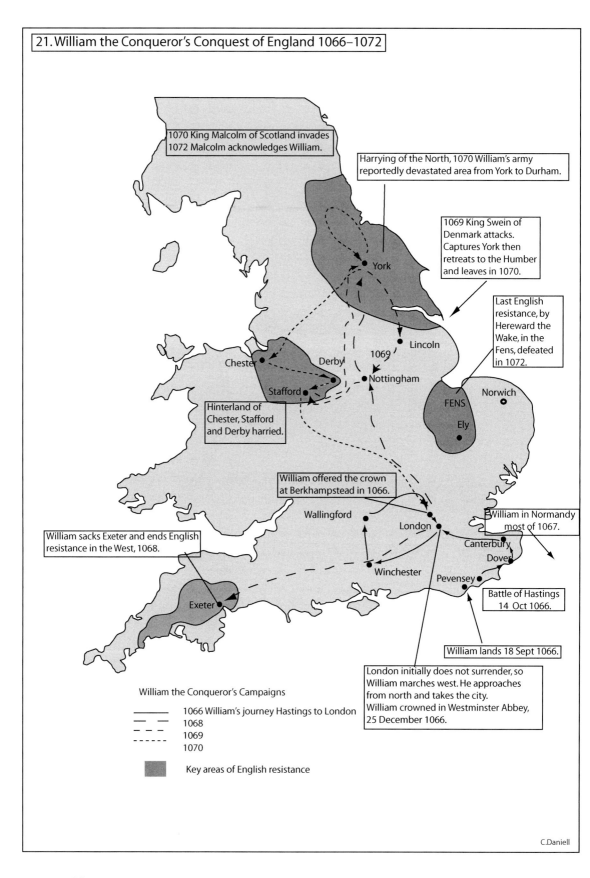

21. William the Conqueror's Conquest of England 1066–1072

1070 King Malcolm of Scotland invades
1072 Malcolm acknowledges William.

Harrying of the North, 1070 William's army reportedly devastated area from York to Durham.

1069 King Swein of Denmark attacks. Captures York then retreats to the Humber and leaves in 1070.

Last English resistance, by Hereward the Wake, in the Fens, defeated in 1072.

York

Lincoln

Chester

Derby

1069

Nottingham

Norwich

Stafford

FENS

Hinterland of Chester, Stafford and Derby harried.

Ely

William offered the crown at Berkhampstead in 1066.

Wallingford

William in Normandy most of 1067.

London

William sacks Exeter and ends English resistance in the West, 1068.

Canterbury

Dover

Winchester

Pevensey

Battle of Hastings 14 Oct 1066.

Exeter

William lands 18 Sept 1066.

London initially does not surrender, so William marches west. He approaches from north and takes the city. William crowned in Westminster Abbey, 25 December 1066.

William the Conqueror's Campaigns

- —— 1066 William's journey Hastings to London
- — — 1068
- — · — 1069
- - - - - 1070

Key areas of English resistance

C.Daniell

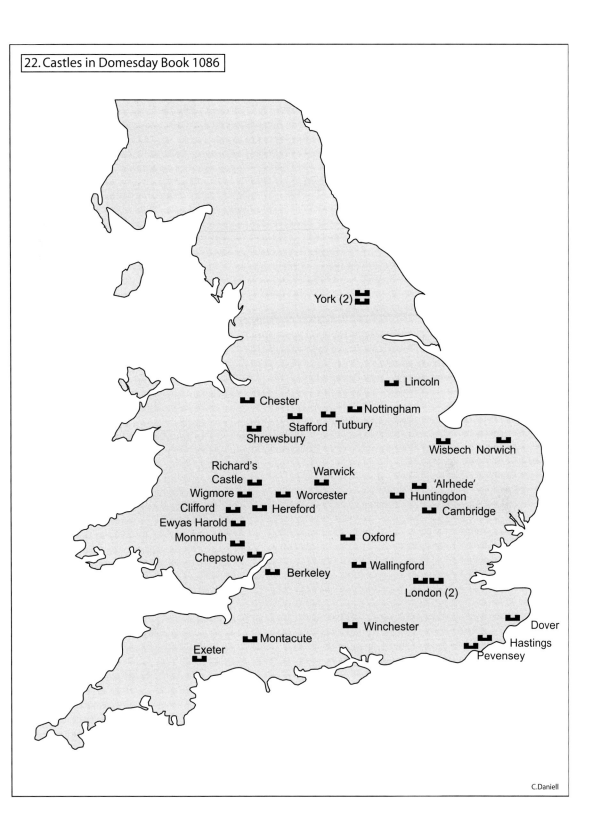

22. Castles in Domesday Book 1086

York (2)

Lincoln

Chester

Nottingham

Stafford Tutbury

Shrewsbury

Wisbech Norwich

Richard's
Castle

Warwick

'Alrhede'

Wigmore

Worcester

Huntingdon

Clifford

Hereford

Cambridge

Ewyas Harold

Monmouth

Oxford

Chepstow

Wallingford

Berkeley

London (2)

Winchester

Dover

Montacute

Hastings

Exeter

Pevensey

C.Daniell

29

The North

Ulster

Airgilla

Breifne

Connaught

Meath

Dublin

Limerick

Leinster

Munster

Wexford

Waterford

Cork

Bannow Bay

● Viking towns

1169 – A Norman force of mercenaries lands at Bannow Bay in support of the deposed King of Leinster. After restoring the king, they conquer lands for themselves, made easier by the lack of a cohesive Irish force. Worried that these lords were independent of the English crown, Henry II, King of England, later invades to impose his own authority. However, the Anglo-Irish lords always remained semi-independent.

C.Daniell

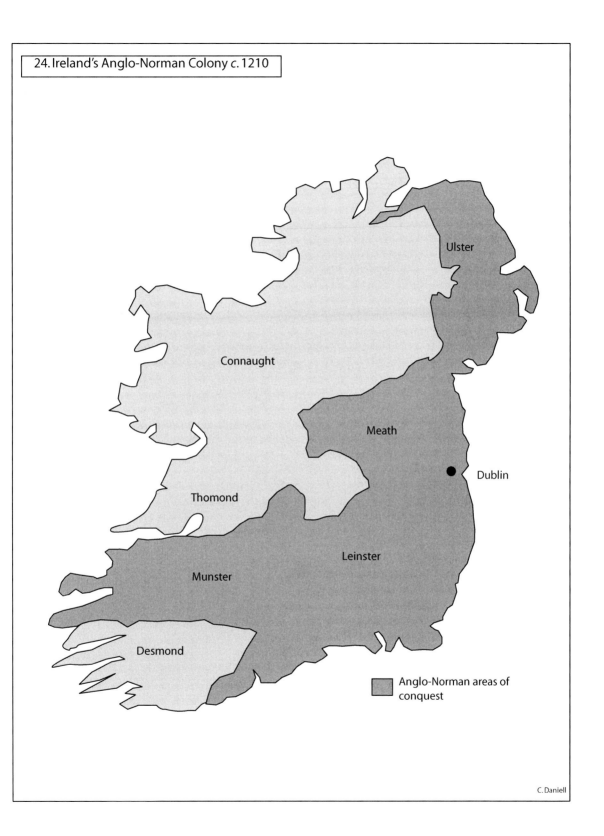

24. Ireland's Anglo-Norman Colony *c.* 1210

Ulster

Connaught

Meath

Dublin

Thomond

Leinster

Munster

Desmond

Anglo-Norman areas of conquest

C. Daniell

31

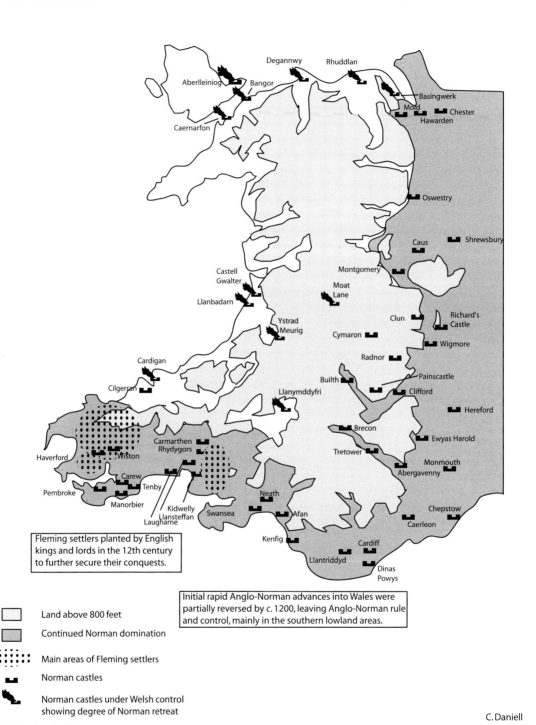

25. Wales c. 1200

Degannwy
Rhuddlan
Aberlleiniog
Bangor
Basingwerk
Mold
Chester
Caernarfon
Hawarden

Oswestry

Caus
Shrewsbury

Castell
Gwalter
Montgomery
Moat
Lane
Llanbadarn
Clun
Richard's
Castle

Ystrad
Meurig
Cymaron
Wigmore

Cardigan
Radnor
Painscastle
Cilgerran
Builth
Clifford

Llanymddyfri
Hereford

Carmarthen
Rhydygors
Brecon
Haverford
Wiston
Tretower
Ewyas Harold

Carew
Monmouth
Pembroke
Tenby
Abergavenny
Manorbier
Kidwelly
Neath
Llansteffan
Swansea
Afan
Chepstow
Laugharne
Caerleon

Kenfig
Cardiff
Llantriddyd
Dinas
Powys

Fleming settlers planted by English
kings and lords in the 12th century
to further secure their conquests.

Initial rapid Anglo-Norman advances into Wales were
partially reversed by c. 1200, leaving Anglo-Norman rule
and control, mainly in the southern lowland areas.

Land above 800 feet

Continued Norman domination

Main areas of Fleming settlers

Norman castles

Norman castles under Welsh control
showing degree of Norman retreat

C. Daniell

32

26. King John's Campaign and the Barons' Revolt 1215–1216

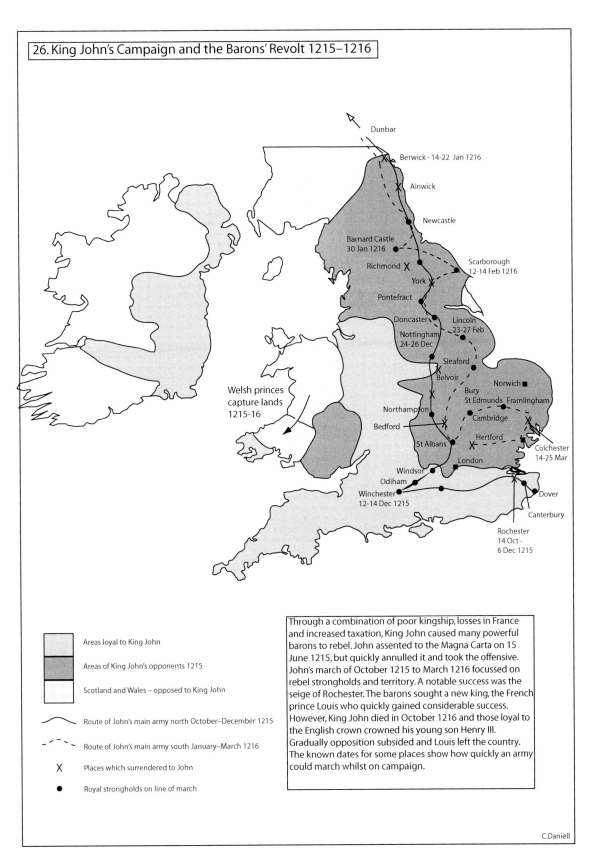

Dunbar

Berwick - 14-22 Jan 1216

Alnwick

Newcastle

Barnard Castle
30 Jan 1216

Richmond

Scarborough
12-14 Feb 1216

York

Pontefract

Doncaster

Lincoln
23-27 Feb

Nottingham
24-26 Dec

Sleaford

Belvoir

Norwich

Welsh princes
capture lands
1215-16

Bury
St Edmunds Framlingham

Northampton

Cambridge

Bedford

Hertford

St Albans

Colchester
14-25 Mar

London

Windsor

Odiham

Dover

Winchester
12-14 Dec 1215

Canterbury

Rochester
14 Oct -
6 Dec 1215

Through a combination of poor kingship, losses in France and increased taxation, King John caused many powerful barons to rebel. John assented to the Magna Carta on 15 June 1215, but quickly annulled it and took the offensive. John's march of October 1215 to March 1216 focussed on rebel strongholds and territory. A notable success was the seige of Rochester. The barons sought a new king, the French prince Louis who quickly gained considerable success. However, King John died in October 1216 and those loyal to the English crown crowned his young son Henry III. Gradually opposition subsided and Louis left the country. The known dates for some places show how quickly an army could march whilst on campaign.

Areas loyal to King John

Areas of King John's opponents 1215

Scotland and Wales – opposed to King John

Route of John's main army north October–December 1215

Route of John's main army south January–March 1216

X   Places which surrendered to John

●   Royal strongholds on line of march

C.Daniell

33

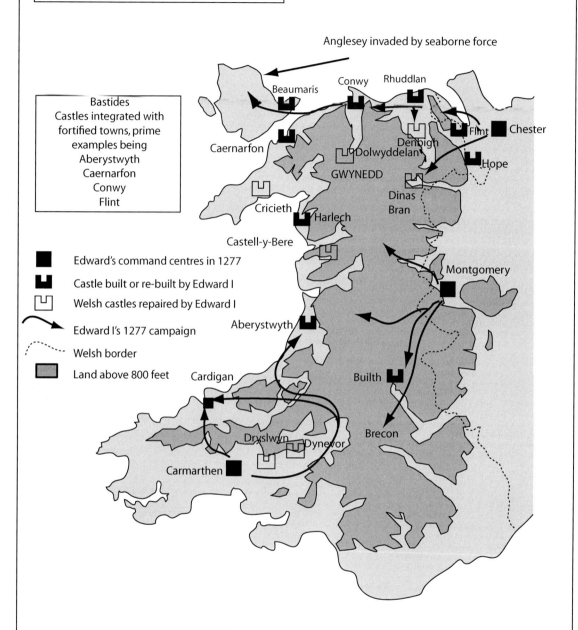

27. Edward I's 1277 Campaign and Castles

Anglesey invaded by seaborne force

Beaumaris

Conwy

Rhuddlan

Chester

Flint

Caernarfon

Denbigh

Dolwyddelan

Hope

GWYNEDD

Dinas
Bran

Cricieth

Harlech

Castell-y-Bere

Montgomery

Aberystwyth

Cardigan

Builth

Dryslwyn

Dynevor

Brecon

Carmarthen

Bastides
Castles integrated with
fortified towns, prime
examples being
Aberystwyth
Caernarfon
Conwy
Flint

■ Edward's command centres in 1277

Castle built or re-built by Edward I

Welsh castles repaired by Edward I

Edward I's 1277 campaign

Welsh border

Land above 800 feet

Edward I's campaign in 1277 against Llywelyn ap Gruffudd, Prince of Wales, was designed to force Llywelyn back to Gwynedd by attacks from Carmarthen, Montgomery and Chester. The tactic worked within a year and Llywelyn surrendered.
The Welsh rose again in 1282–3, but Edward followed a similar tactic and the Welsh were crushed. Edward secured his victories by a major programme of castle building.

C.Daniell

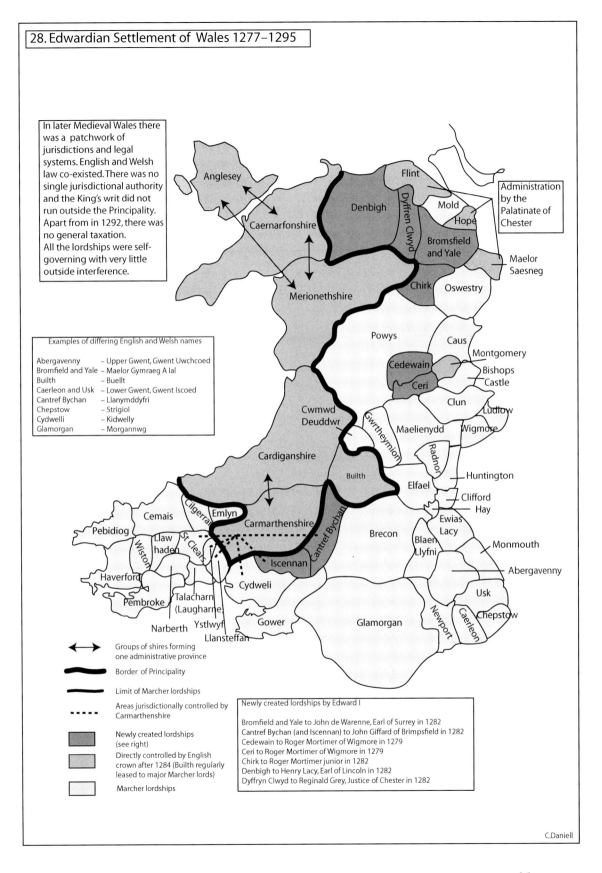

28. Edwardian Settlement of Wales 1277–1295

In later Medieval Wales there was a patchwork of jurisdictions and legal systems. English and Welsh law co-existed. There was no single jurisdictional authority and the King's writ did not run outside the Principality. Apart from in 1292, there was no general taxation. All the lordships were self-governing with very little outside interference.

Administration by the Palatinate of Chester

Examples of differing English and Welsh names

Abergavenny	– Upper Gwent, Gwent Uwchcoed
Bromfield and Yale	– Maelor Gymraeg A Ial
Builth	– Buellt
Caerleon and Usk	– Lower Gwent, Gwent Iscoed
Cantref Bychan	– Llanymddyfri
Chepstow	– Strigoil
Cydwelli	– Kidwelly
Glamorgan	– Morgannwg

Anglesey
Flint
Denbigh
Mold
Hope
Dyffren Clwyd
Caernarfonshire
Bromsfield and Yale
Maelor Saesneg
Chirk
Oswestry
Merionethshire
Powys
Caus
Montgomery
Cedewain
Bishops Castle
Ceri
Clun
Ludlow
Cwmwd Deuddwr
Gwrtheyrnion
Maelienydd
Wigmore
Cardiganshire
Radnor
Builth
Huntington
Elfael
Clifford
Hay
Cilgerran
Emlyn
Cemais
Carmarthenshire
Ewias Lacy
Brecon
Pebidiog
Llawhaden
St Clears
Cantref Bychan
Blaen Llyfni
Monmouth
Wiston
Iscennan
Abergavenny
Haverford
Cydweli
Pembroke
Talacharn (Laugharne)
Ystlwyf
Usk
Newport
Caerleon
Chepstow
Narberth
Llansteffan
Gower
Glamorgan

Groups of shires forming one administrative province

Border of Principality

Limit of Marcher lordships

Areas jurisdictionally controlled by Carmarthenshire

Newly created lordships (see right)

Directly controlled by English crown after 1284 (Builth regularly leased to major Marcher lords)

Marcher lordships

Newly created lordships by Edward I

Bromfield and Yale to John de Warenne, Earl of Surrey in 1282
Cantref Bychan (and Iscennan) to John Giffard of Brimpsfield in 1282
Cedewain to Roger Mortimer of Wigmore in 1279
Ceri to Roger Mortimer of Wigmore in 1279
Chirk to Roger Mortimer junior in 1282
Denbigh to Henry Lacy, Earl of Lincoln in 1282
Dyffryn Clwyd to Reginald Grey, Justice of Chester in 1282

C. Daniell

35

29. Power in Wales 1322–1326

Anglesey

Flint

Denbigh

Dyffren Clwyd

Mold

Hope

Caernarfonshire

Bromsfield and Yale

Maelor Saesneg

Chirk

Oswestry

Merionethshire

Powys

Caus

Montgomery

Wales was a patchwork of lordships.
Ruthless nobles who were royal favourites
could quickly build up substantial
landholdings. The Despensers, father and
son, rapidly gained a large number of Welsh
lordships from 1317 until their downfall in
1326. Their Welsh lands had an estimated
worth of £5,000 a year.

Cedewain

Bishops Castle

Ceri

Clun

Cwmwd
Deuddwr

Ludlow

Maelienydd

Wigmore

Gwrtheyrnion

Cardiganshire

Radnor

Builth

Huntington

Elfael

Clifford

Hay

Cilgerran

Emlyn

Cemais

Cantref Bychan

Ewias
Lacy

Pebidiog

Caermarthenshire

Brecon

Monmouth

Llaw
haden

St Clears

Blaen
Llyfni

Wiston

Iscennan

Abergavenny

Haverford

Cydweli

Usk

Pembroke

Newport

Caerleon

Narberth

Ystlwyf

Gower

Glamorgan

Chepstow

Talacharn
(Laugharne)

Llansteffan

Border of Principality

Under royal control

Held by Despensers (all held
by younger Despenser except for
Denbigh held by elder Despenser)

Lands of Earl of Arundel

Other lordships

After R.R. Davies, *The Age of Conquest, Wales 1063–1415*, Oxford University Press, 1991

C.Daniell

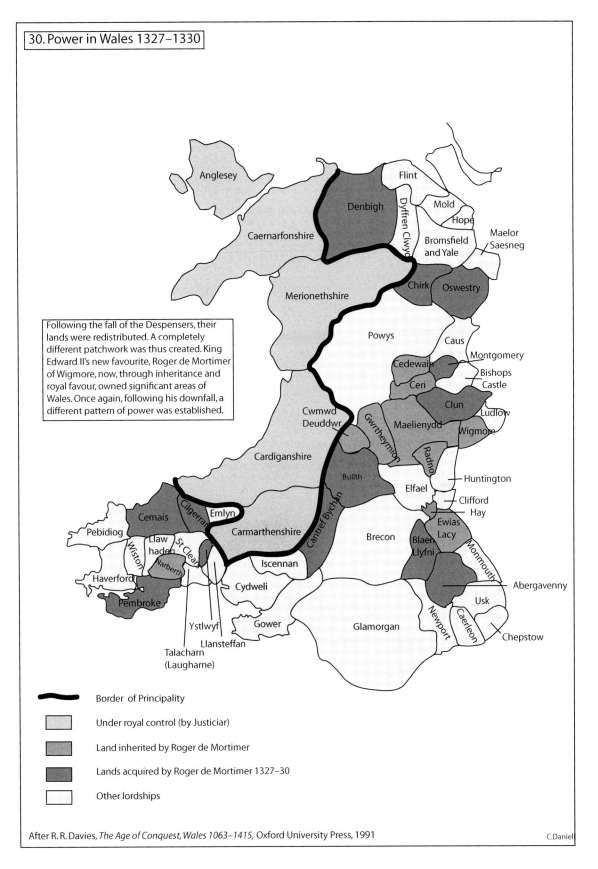

30. Power in Wales 1327–1330

Anglesey

Flint

Denbigh

Dyffren Clwyd

Mold

Hope

Maelor Saesneg

Caernarfonshire

Bromsfield and Yale

Merionethshire

Chirk

Oswestry

Following the fall of the Despensers, their lands were redistributed. A completely different patchwork was thus created. King Edward II's new favourite, Roger de Mortimer of Wigmore, now, through inheritance and royal favour, owned significant areas of Wales. Once again, following his downfall, a different pattern of power was established.

Powys

Caus

Montgomery

Cedewain

Bishops Castle

Ceri

Clun

Ludlow

Cwmwd Deuddwr

Gwrtheyrnion

Maelienydd

Wigmore

Cardiganshire

Radnor

Builth

Huntington

Elfael

Clifford

Hay

Cilgerran

Emlyn

Cemais

Carmarthenshire

Cantref Bychan

Brecon

Ewias Lacy

Blaen Llyfni

Monmouth

Pebidiog

Llaw haden

St Clears

Narberth

Iscennan

Abergavenny

Haverford

Cydweli

Usk

Pembroke

Caerleon

Ystlwyf

Gower

Glamorgan

Newport

Chepstow

Llansteffan

Talacharn (Laugharne)

Border of Principality

Under royal control (by Justiciar)

Land inherited by Roger de Mortimer

Lands acquired by Roger de Mortimer 1327–30

Other lordships

After R. R. Davies, *The Age of Conquest, Wales 1063–1415*, Oxford University Press, 1991

C.Daniell

37

31. Edward I's Scottish Campaign 1296

⊗ Battle – English victory

Banff
Elgin
Rothes
Kildrummy
Aberdeen
Glenbervie
Brechin
Kincardine
Montrose
Forfar
Farnell
Clunie
Dundee
Arbroath
Perth
St Andrews
Stirling
Dunfermline
Haddington
Linlithgow
Battle of Dunbar 27 April 1296
Edinburgh
Berwick
Lauder
Carlisle

Edward I started the campaign at Berwick, March 1296.

Edward I finished the campaign at Berwick, 22 August 1296.

Edward I attacked Scotland in March 1296 after Edward's puppet king, John Balliol, renounced his allegiance to Edward. Edward defeated the Scottish army at Dunbar and thereafter marched almost unopposed through Scotland.

C.Daniell

32. Robert Bruce's recovery of Scotland 1307–1318

○ Major castles captured for Bruce 1307–1309

● Major castles captured for Bruce 1312–1318

⊗ Battle – Scottish victory

⊗ Battle – English victory

Area of northern England subject to Scottish raids

Nairn (1307)

Elgin (1308)   Banff (1310?)

Inverness (1307)

Aberdeen (1308)

Forfar (1308)

Declaration of Arbroath 1320
A declaration of independence from English power by Scottish nobility.

Dundee (1312)
Perth (1313)   Arbroath

Dumbarton (1309)
Stirling (1314)   St Andrews

Bannockburn
(23-24 June 1314)

Edinburgh (1314)   Berwick (1318)

Ayr (1313)   Roxburgh (1314)

Dumfries (1313)

Scottish Raids
1311, 1316, 1319,
1322, 1327

York.
Scottish army reaches city gates in 1322.

Myton on Swale (1319)

Many Scottish nobles fought against Edward I's rule and Robert Bruce was crowned King of Scots in 1306. Edward I died in 1307 and his son Edward II was a poor military leader. Robert Bruce recovered land and castles from the English in two main phases of campaigning and raided across the north of England. The English recognised Scottish independence in 1328.

C.Daniell

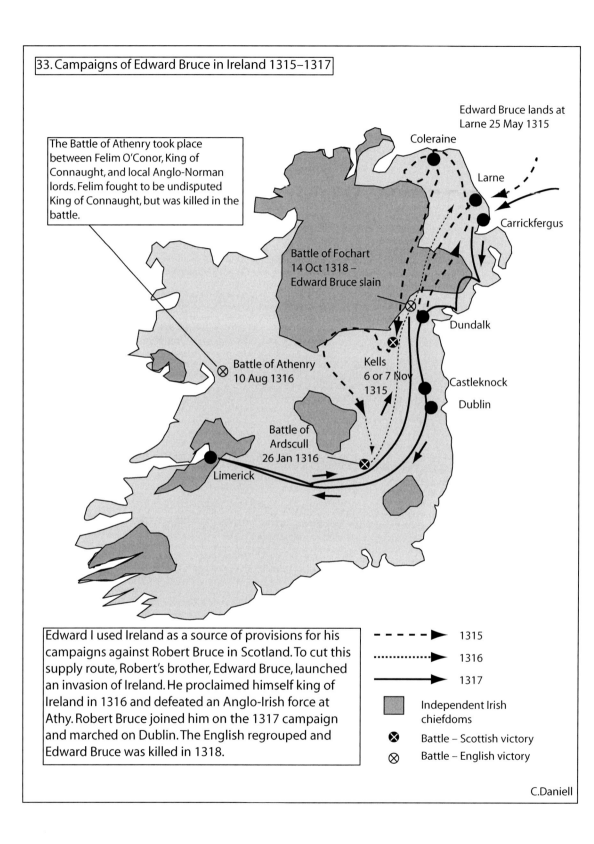

33. Campaigns of Edward Bruce in Ireland 1315–1317

Edward Bruce lands at
Larne 25 May 1315

Coleraine

Larne

Carrickfergus

The Battle of Athenry took place
between Felim O'Conor, King of
Connaught, and local Anglo-Norman
lords. Felim fought to be undisputed
King of Connaught, but was killed in the
battle.

Battle of Fochart
14 Oct 1318 –
Edward Bruce slain

Dundalk

Battle of Athenry
10 Aug 1316

Kells
6 or 7 Nov
1315

Castleknock

Dublin

Battle of
Ardscull
26 Jan 1316

Limerick

Edward I used Ireland as a source of provisions for his
campaigns against Robert Bruce in Scotland. To cut this
supply route, Robert's brother, Edward Bruce, launched
an invasion of Ireland. He proclaimed himself king of
Ireland in 1316 and defeated an Anglo-Irish force at
Athy. Robert Bruce joined him on the 1317 campaign
and marched on Dublin. The English regrouped and
Edward Bruce was killed in 1318.

- - - ▶ 1315
·········▶ 1316
———▶ 1317

Independent Irish
chiefdoms

⊗ Battle – Scottish victory
⊗ Battle – English victory

C. Daniell

40

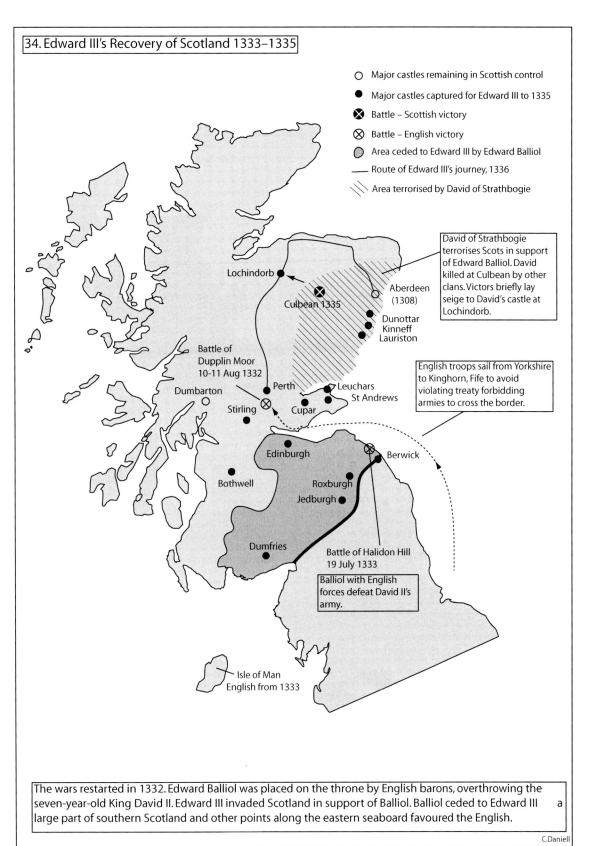

34. Edward III's Recovery of Scotland 1333–1335

○ Major castles remaining in Scottish control

● Major castles captured for Edward III to 1335

⊗ Battle – Scottish victory

⊗ Battle – English victory

Area ceded to Edward III by Edward Balliol

— Route of Edward III's journey, 1336

Area terrorised by David of Strathbogie

David of Strathbogie terrorises Scots in support of Edward Balliol. David killed at Culbean by other clans. Victors briefly lay seige to David's castle at Lochindorb.

Lochindorb

Aberdeen (1308)

Culbean 1335

Dunottar
Kinneff
Lauriston

Battle of Dupplin Moor 10-11 Aug 1332

Dumbarton

Perth

Leuchars
St Andrews

Stirling

Cupar

English troops sail from Yorkshire to Kinghorn, Fife to avoid violating treaty forbidding armies to cross the border.

Edinburgh

Berwick

Bothwell

Roxburgh

Jedburgh

Dumfries

Battle of Halidon Hill 19 July 1333

Balliol with English forces defeat David II's army.

Isle of Man
English from 1333

The wars restarted in 1332. Edward Balliol was placed on the throne by English barons, overthrowing the seven-year-old King David II. Edward III invaded Scotland in support of Balliol. Balliol ceded to Edward III a large part of southern Scotland and other points along the eastern seaboard favoured the English.

C.Daniell

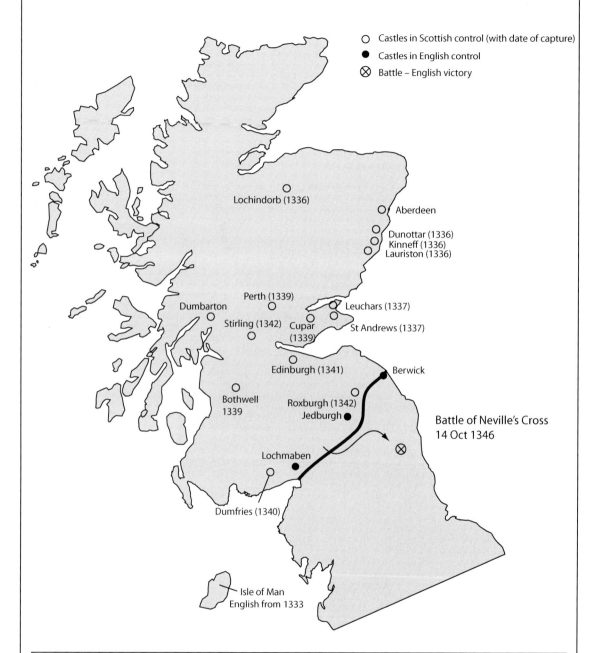

35. Scottish Recovery 1335–1356

○ Castles in Scottish control (with date of capture)
● Castles in English control
⊗ Battle – English victory

Lochindorb (1336)

Aberdeen

Dunottar (1336)
Kinneff (1336)
Lauriston (1336)

Perth (1339)
Dumbarton
Leuchars (1337)
Stirling (1342) Cupar
(1339)
St Andrews (1337)

Edinburgh (1341)
Berwick

Bothwell
1339
Roxburgh (1342)
Jedburgh ●

**Battle of Neville's Cross
14 Oct 1346**

Lochmaben ●

Dumfries (1340)

Isle of Man
English from 1333

After the English victory at Halidon Hill in 1333, David II escaped to France, returning in 1341. In the meantime the Scottish nobles had continued fighting against the Balliol faction and achieved considerable successes, winning back many towns and castles. David II planned an attack on Durham, but was defeated at Neville's Cross. David II was captured and ransomed. Edward III launched a campaign of destruction on southern Scotland in 1356. However, later in the year the French king was captured at Poitiers. Isolated, David II accepted a ten-year truce.

C. Daniell

36. Border Battles in the Hundred Years War – Battles of Halidon Hill, Otterburn and Neville's Cross

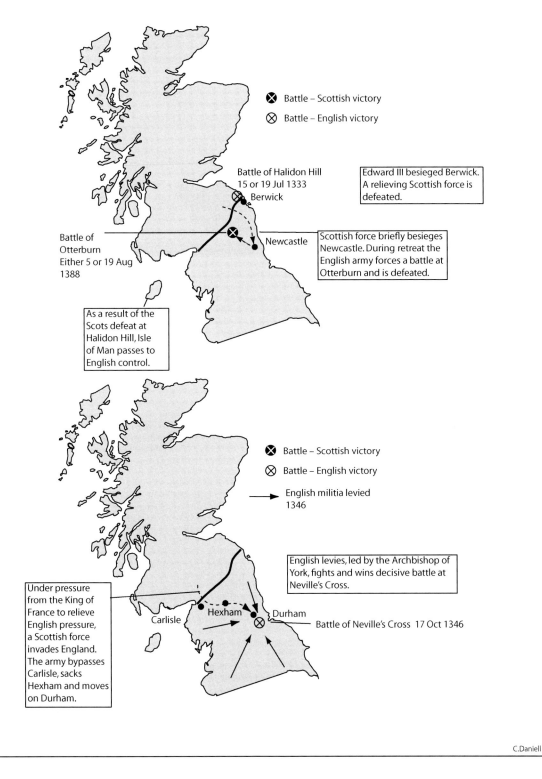

Battle – Scottish victory

Battle – English victory

Battle of Halidon Hill
15 or 19 Jul 1333
Berwick

Edward III besieged Berwick. A relieving Scottish force is defeated.

Battle of Otterburn Either 5 or 19 Aug 1388

Newcastle

Scottish force briefly besieges Newcastle. During retreat the English army forces a battle at Otterburn and is defeated.

As a result of the Scots defeat at Halidon Hill, Isle of Man passes to English control.

Battle – Scottish victory

Battle – English victory

English militia levied 1346

English levies, led by the Archbishop of York, fights and wins decisive battle at Neville's Cross.

Under pressure from the King of France to relieve English pressure, a Scottish force invades England. The army bypasses Carlisle, sacks Hexham and moves on Durham.

Carlisle   Hexham   Durham

Battle of Neville's Cross 17 Oct 1346

C.Daniell

43

37. The Lordship of the Isles

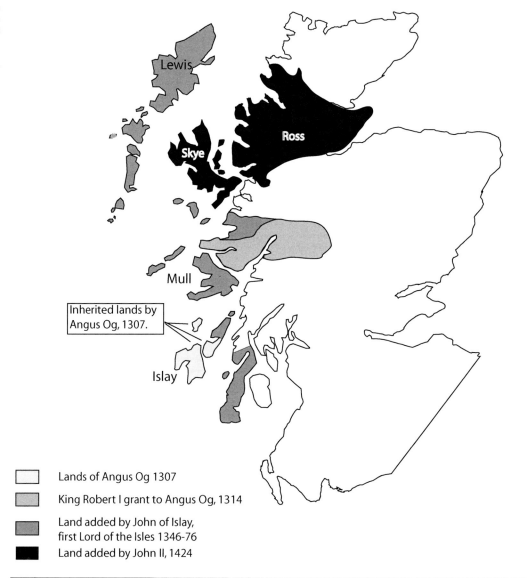

Lewis

Ross

Skye

Mull

Inherited lands by
Angus Og, 1307.

Islay

☐ Lands of Angus Og 1307

▨ King Robert I grant to Angus Og, 1314

▨ Land added by John of Islay,
first Lord of the Isles 1346-76

■ Land added by John II, 1424

The leadership of the Lordship of the Isles remained with one family over four generations. At the height of their power they controlled the western isles and areas of northern Scotland. The lordship collapsed after 1475 because John II had made a treaty with the English King Edward IV to overthrow the King of Scotland. When this became known many of his lands were forfeited. The Lordship itself was governed in four separate parts (based on the islands of Lewis, Skye, Mull and Islay) and consisted of many separate clans.

C.Daniell

44

38. Peasants' Revolt 1381

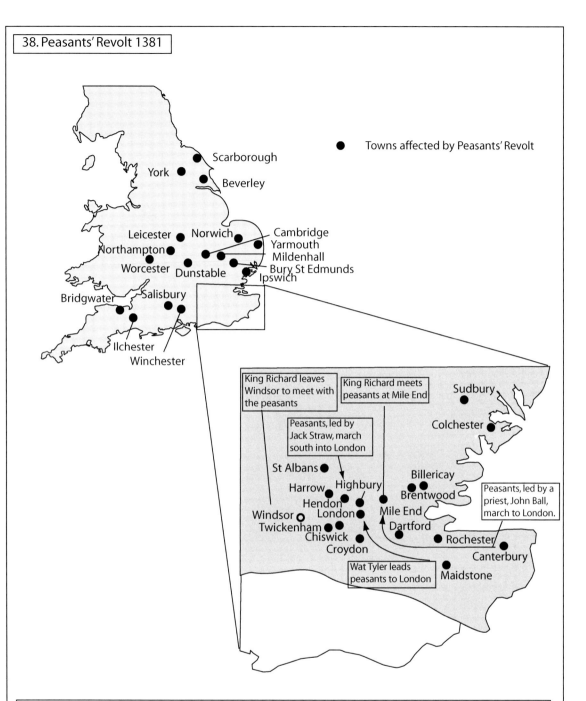

● Towns affected by Peasants' Revolt

Scarborough
York
Beverley
Leicester Norwich Cambridge
Northampton Yarmouth
Worcester Mildenhall
Dunstable Bury St Edmunds
Ipswich
Bridgwater Salisbury
Ilchester
Winchester

King Richard leaves Windsor to meet with the peasants

King Richard meets peasants at Mile End

Peasants, led by Jack Straw, march south into London

Sudbury
Colchester
St Albans
Billericay
Harrow Highbury
Brentwood
Hendon
Windsor London Mile End
Twickenham Dartford
Chiswick
Croydon Rochester
Canterbury
Maidstone

Peasants, led by a priest, John Ball, march to London.

Wat Tyler leads peasants to London

The revolt came about because of the combined influences of the third national Poll Tax in 4 years (1377, 1379 and 1381). The Poll Tax was based on taxation for everyone, except the very poorest.
The 1381 tax, combined with a collapse in population after the 1349–50 outbreak of the Black Death and landlords who were seen to be oppressive, led to the Revolt.
The most dangerous occurrence to the State was the rebel march from Kent into London, led by Wat Tyler and John Ball. The young King Richard II met the rebels and granted their petition, but once the rebels dispersed Richard rescinded it.
Targetted reprisals followed, but the Poll Tax did not continue.

C.Daniell

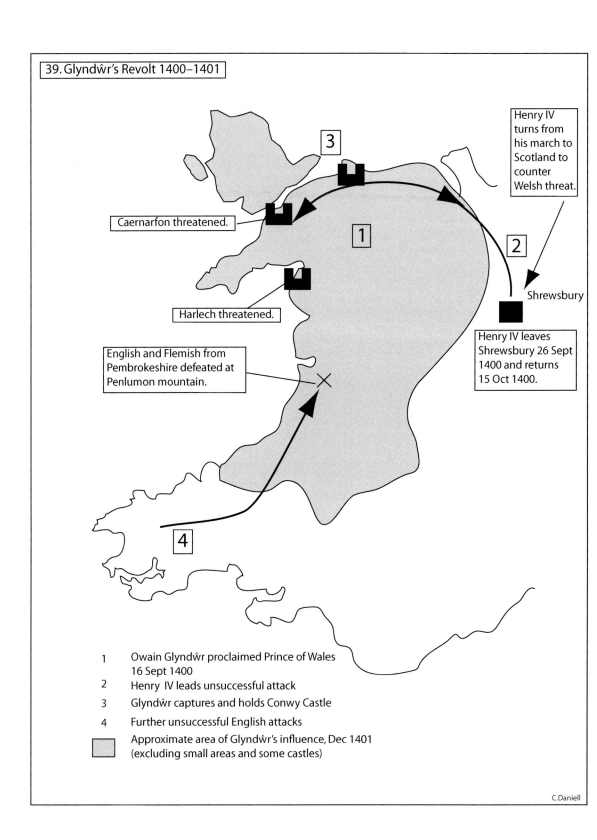

39. Glyndŵr's Revolt 1400–1401

Henry IV turns from his march to Scotland to counter Welsh threat.

3

Caernarfon threatened.

1

2

Harlech threatened.

Shrewsbury

Henry IV leaves Shrewsbury 26 Sept 1400 and returns 15 Oct 1400.

English and Flemish from Pembrokeshire defeated at Penlumon mountain.

4

1   Owain Glyndŵr proclaimed Prince of Wales
      16 Sept 1400
2   Henry IV leads unsuccessful attack
3   Glyndŵr captures and holds Conwy Castle
4   Further unsuccessful English attacks
      Approximate area of Glyndŵr's influence, Dec 1401
      (excluding small areas and some castles)

C.Daniell

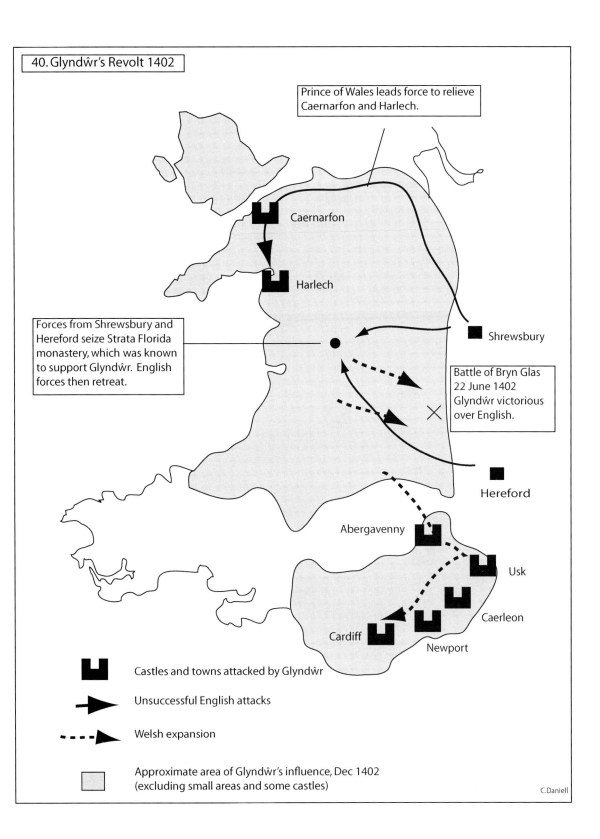

40. Glyndŵr's Revolt 1402

Prince of Wales leads force to relieve Caernarfon and Harlech.

Caernarfon

Harlech

Shrewsbury

Forces from Shrewsbury and Hereford seize Strata Florida monastery, which was known to support Glyndŵr. English forces then retreat.

Battle of Bryn Glas
22 June 1402
Glyndŵr victorious over English.

Hereford

Abergavenny

Usk

Caerleon

Cardiff

Newport

Castles and towns attacked by Glyndŵr

Unsuccessful English attacks

Welsh expansion

Approximate area of Glyndŵr's influence, Dec 1402 (excluding small areas and some castles)

C.Daniell

47

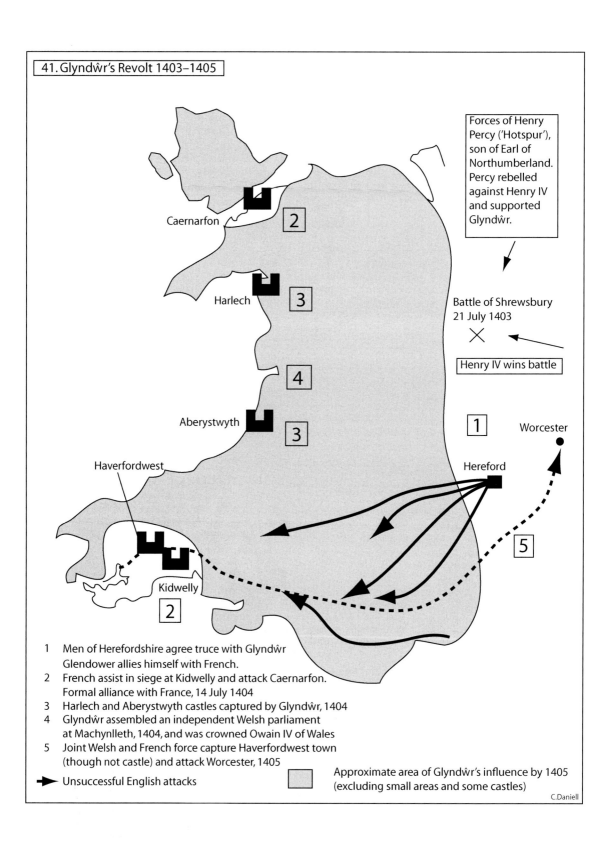

41. Glyndŵr's Revolt 1403–1405

Forces of Henry Percy ('Hotspur'), son of Earl of Northumberland. Percy rebelled against Henry IV and supported Glyndŵr.

Battle of Shrewsbury 21 July 1403

Henry IV wins battle

Caernarfon

Harlech

Aberystwyth

Haverfordwest

Kidwelly

Worcester

Hereford

1. Men of Herefordshire agree truce with Glyndŵr Glendower allies himself with French.
2. French assist in siege at Kidwelly and attack Caernarfon. Formal alliance with France, 14 July 1404
3. Harlech and Aberystwyth castles captured by Glyndŵr, 1404
4. Glyndŵr assembled an independent Welsh parliament at Machynlleth, 1404, and was crowned Owain IV of Wales
5. Joint Welsh and French force capture Haverfordwest town (though not castle) and attack Worcester, 1405

➤ Unsuccessful English attacks

Approximate area of Glyndŵr's influence by 1405 (excluding small areas and some castles)

C.Daniell

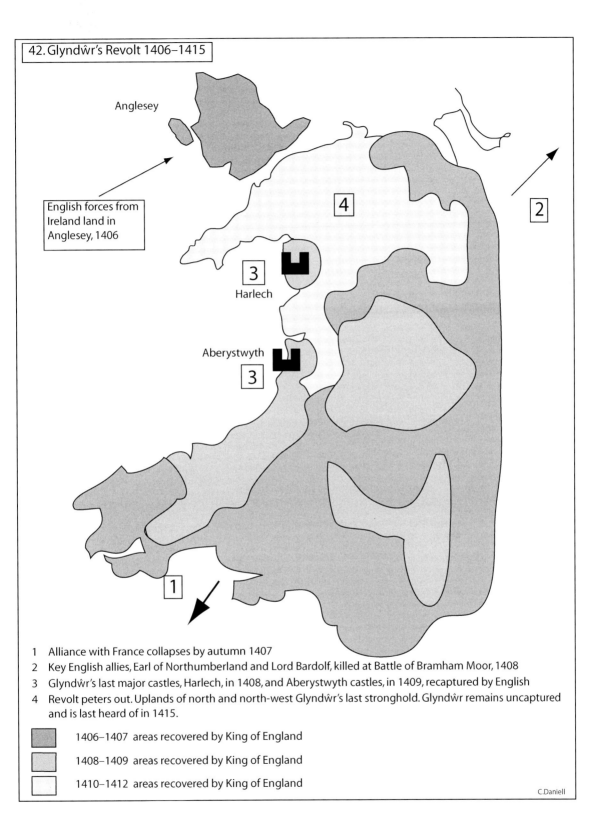

42. Glyndŵr's Revolt 1406–1415

Anglesey

English forces from Ireland land in Anglesey, 1406

4

2

3

Harlech

Aberystwyth

3

1

1   Alliance with France collapses by autumn 1407
2   Key English allies, Earl of Northumberland and Lord Bardolf, killed at Battle of Bramham Moor, 1408
3   Glyndŵr's last major castles, Harlech, in 1408, and Aberystwyth castles, in 1409, recaptured by English
4   Revolt peters out. Uplands of north and north-west Glyndŵr's last stronghold. Glyndŵr remains uncaptured and is last heard of in 1415.

1406–1407 areas recovered by King of England

1408–1409 areas recovered by King of England

1410–1412 areas recovered by King of England

C.Daniell

49

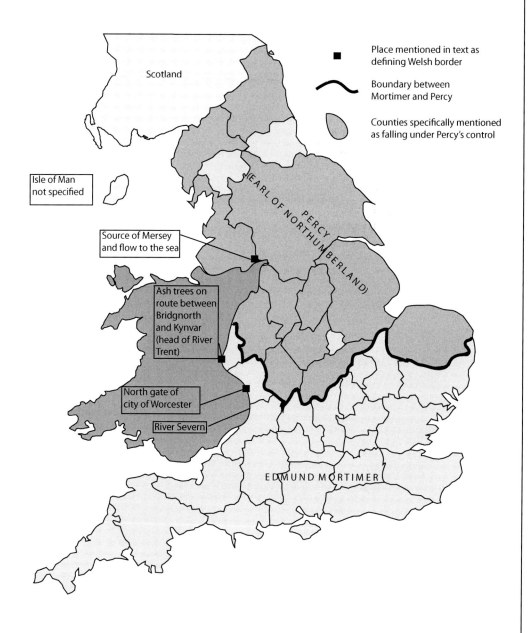

43. Glyndŵr's Proposed Tripartite Division of England and Wales 1405

Scotland

■ Place mentioned in text as defining Welsh border

⌢ Boundary between Mortimer and Percy

Counties specifically mentioned as falling under Percy's control

Isle of Man not specified

Source of Mersey and flow to the sea

PERCY (EARL OF NORTHUMBERLAND)

Ash trees on route between Bridgnorth and Kynvar (head of River Trent)

North gate of city of Worcester

River Severn

EDMUND MORTIMER

The Tripartite Agreement was agreed between Owain Glyndŵr, Edmund Mortimer and the Earl of Northumberland in 1405 to divide England and Wales once Henry IV had been overthrown. Henry IV was victorious, but the plan showed the aspirations of the rebels.

C.Daniell

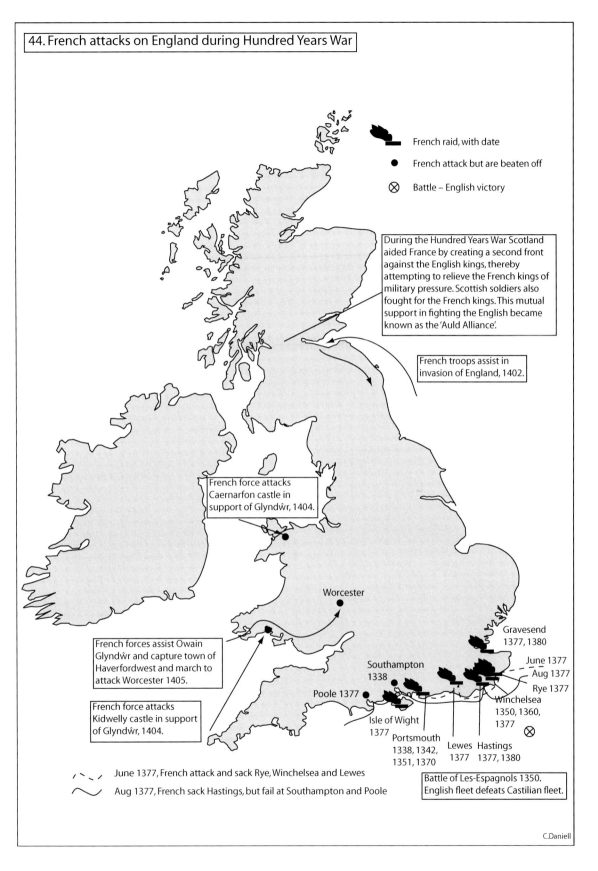

44. French attacks on England during Hundred Years War

French raid, with date

French attack but are beaten off

⊗ Battle – English victory

During the Hundred Years War Scotland aided France by creating a second front against the English kings, thereby attempting to relieve the French kings of military pressure. Scottish soldiers also fought for the French kings. This mutual support in fighting the English became known as the 'Auld Alliance'.

French troops assist in invasion of England, 1402.

French force attacks Caernarfon castle in support of Glyndŵr, 1404.

Worcester

French forces assist Owain Glyndŵr and capture town of Haverfordwest and march to attack Worcester 1405.

French force attacks Kidwelly castle in support of Glyndŵr, 1404.

Gravesend 1377, 1380

June 1377

Aug 1377

Rye 1377

Winchelsea 1350, 1360, 1377

Southampton 1338

Poole 1377

Isle of Wight 1377

Portsmouth 1338, 1342, 1351, 1370

Lewes 1377

Hastings 1377, 1380

⊗

June 1377, French attack and sack Rye, Winchelsea and Lewes

Aug 1377, French sack Hastings, but fail at Southampton and Poole

Battle of Les-Espagnols 1350. English fleet defeats Castilian fleet.

C.Daniell

51

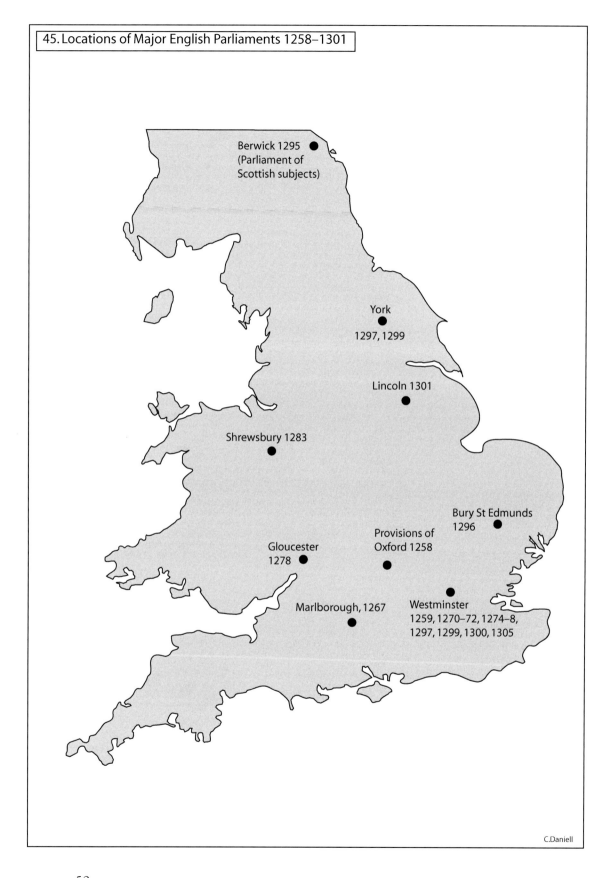

45. Locations of Major English Parliaments 1258–1301

Berwick 1295
(Parliament of
Scottish subjects)

York
1297, 1299

Lincoln 1301

Shrewsbury 1283

Bury St Edmunds
1296

Provisions of
Oxford 1258

Gloucester
1278

Marlborough, 1267

Westminster
1259, 1270–72, 1274–8,
1297, 1299, 1300, 1305

C.Daniell

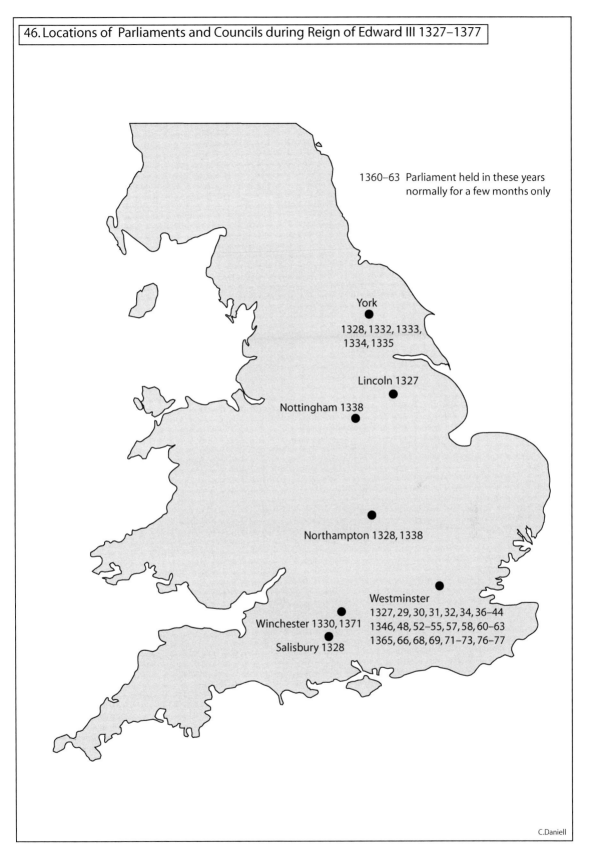

46. Locations of Parliaments and Councils during Reign of Edward III 1327–1377

1360–63 Parliament held in these years
normally for a few months only

York
1328, 1332, 1333,
1334, 1335

Lincoln 1327

Nottingham 1338

Northampton 1328, 1338

Westminster
1327, 29, 30, 31, 32, 34, 36–44
1346, 48, 52–55, 57, 58, 60–63
1365, 66, 68, 69, 71–73, 76–77

Winchester 1330, 1371

Salisbury 1328

C. Daniell

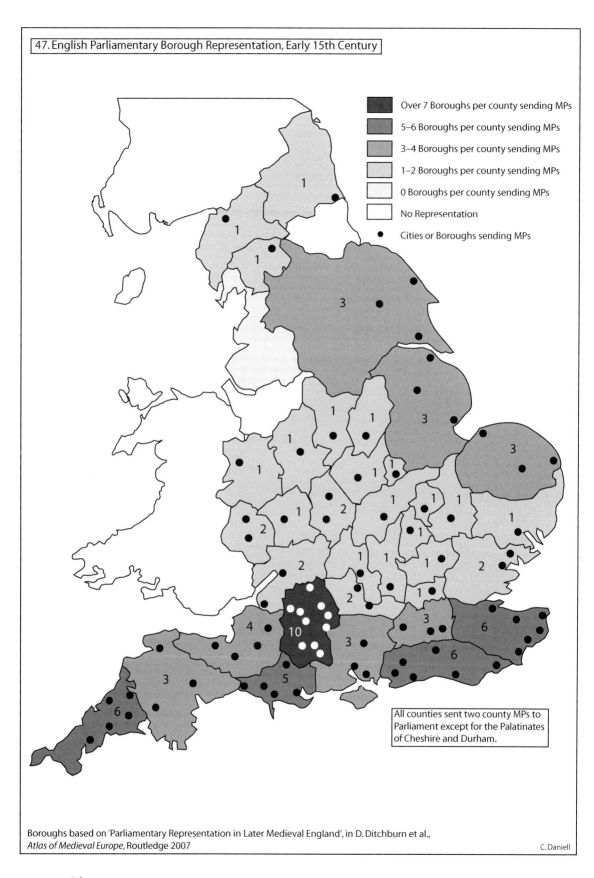

47. English Parliamentary Borough Representation, Early 15th Century

Over 7 Boroughs per county sending MPs

5–6 Boroughs per county sending MPs

3–4 Boroughs per county sending MPs

1–2 Boroughs per county sending MPs

0 Boroughs per county sending MPs

No Representation

● Cities or Boroughs sending MPs

All counties sent two county MPs to Parliament except for the Palatinates of Cheshire and Durham.

Boroughs based on 'Parliamentary Representation in Later Medieval England', in D. Ditchburn et al., *Atlas of Medieval Europe*, Routledge 2007

C. Daniell

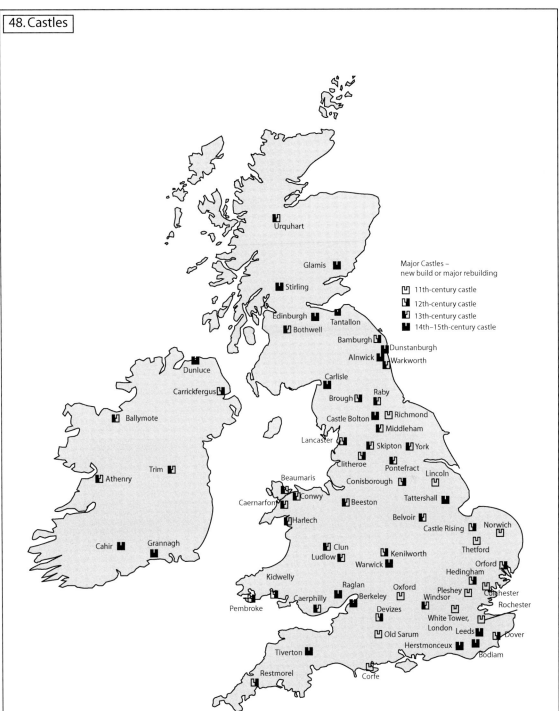

Major Castles –
new build or major rebuilding

- 11th-century castle
- 12th-century castle
- 13th-century castle
- 14th–15th-century castle

Castles were introduced into England by the Normans and changed the nature of defence from the community defence (fortified towns) of the Anglo-Saxons to a single lord's fort. A handful, such as the White Tower in London, were stone, but the majority of Norman castles were originally wood. The classic Norman design was a motte and bailey castle (a mound with fortified enclosure). Over the centuries major castles were rebuilt in stone and their defences updated and made more imposing. Some of the most impressive castles were built by Edward I in order to ensure his Welsh conquests. Castles became obsolete after the development of gunpowder, and a more peaceful country meant comfortable houses became increasingly fashionable.

C. Daniell

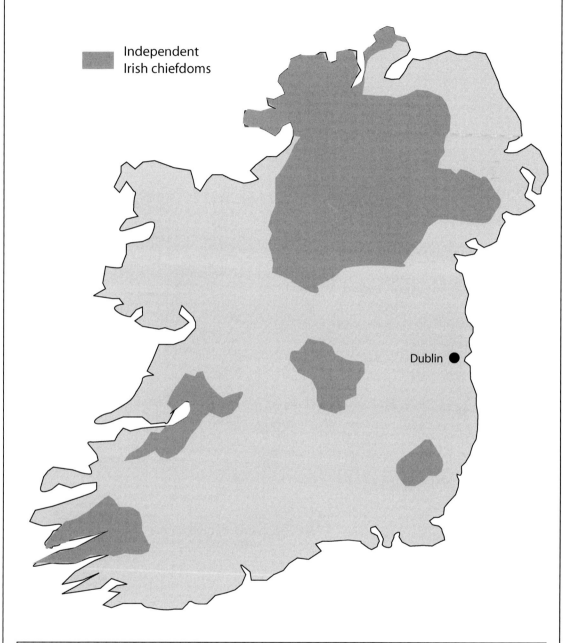

49. Ireland – Areas Under English Authority 1300

Independent
Irish chiefdoms

Dublin ●

By c. 1300 Anglo-Norman lords dominated the majority of Ireland and there were few areas which lay beyond royal authority. However, the lords' own political interests and competitiveness meant there was very little political cohesion between them. In the 14th century the Gaelic-Irish lords were ascendent and reversed the previous Anglo-Norman dominance by military incursion. The Anglo-Norman lords also became culturally integrated into the Gaelic-Irish world, marrying into Gaelic-Irish families. Thus from being 'Anglo-Norman' they became 'Anglo-Irish' and so royal authority from England became greatly diminished as the century progressed, leaving a region round Dublin, known as the 'Pale' as the remnant of the previous widespread authority.

C. Daniell

50. The English Pale in Ireland

Dundalk

Ardee

Kells

Kilcock

Clane

Naas

Dublin

By the end of the 15th century the English crown had lost control over the greater part of Ireland, largely because the previously loyal Anglo-Norman nobles had become 'gaelicised'. The only significant territory still loyal to England was around Dublin and was known as the Pale. In 1494 or 1495 an attempt was made to enclose the area with a great earthen barrier. This does not seem to have been finished.

C.Daniell

51. Burial Places of the Rulers of England 1066–1485

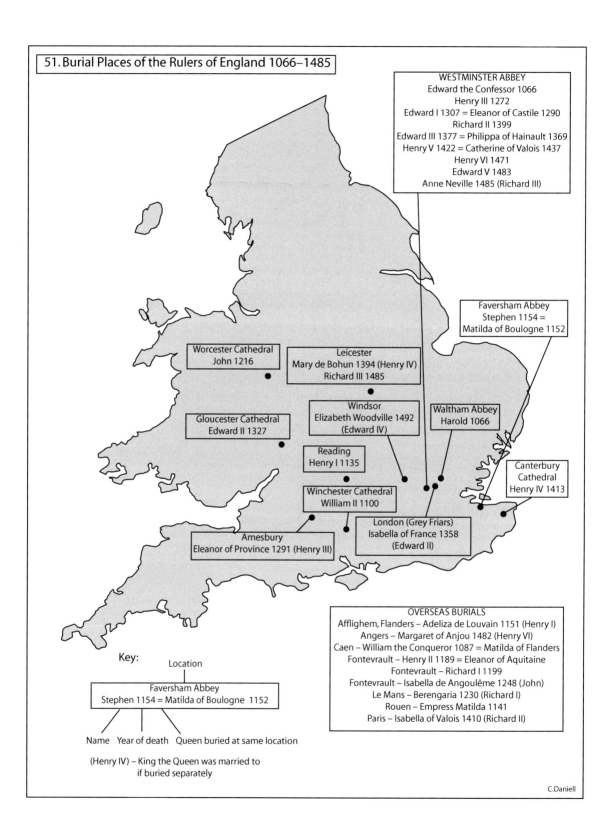

WESTMINSTER ABBEY
Edward the Confessor 1066
Henry III 1272
Edward I 1307 = Eleanor of Castile 1290
Richard II 1399
Edward III 1377 = Philippa of Hainault 1369
Henry V 1422 = Catherine of Valois 1437
Henry VI 1471
Edward V 1483
Anne Neville 1485 (Richard III)

Faversham Abbey
Stephen 1154 =
Matilda of Boulogne 1152

Worcester Cathedral
John 1216

Leicester
Mary de Bohun 1394 (Henry IV)
Richard III 1485

Waltham Abbey
Harold 1066

Windsor
Elizabeth Woodville 1492
(Edward IV)

Gloucester Cathedral
Edward II 1327

Canterbury Cathedral
Henry IV 1413

Reading
Henry I 1135

Winchester Cathedral
William II 1100

London (Grey Friars)
Isabella of France 1358
(Edward II)

Amesbury
Eleanor of Province 1291 (Henry III)

OVERSEAS BURIALS
Afflighem, Flanders – Adeliza de Louvain 1151 (Henry I)
Angers – Margaret of Anjou 1482 (Henry VI)
Caen – William the Conqueror 1087 = Matilda of Flanders
Fontevrault – Henry II 1189 = Eleanor of Aquitaine
Fontevrault – Richard I 1199
Fontevrault – Isabella de Angoulême 1248 (John)
Le Mans – Berengaria 1230 (Richard I)
Rouen – Empress Matilda 1141
Paris – Isabella of Valois 1410 (Richard II)

Key:

Location

Faversham Abbey
Stephen 1154 = Matilda of Boulogne 1152

Name   Year of death   Queen buried at same location

(Henry IV) – King the Queen was married to
        if buried separately

C.Daniell

58

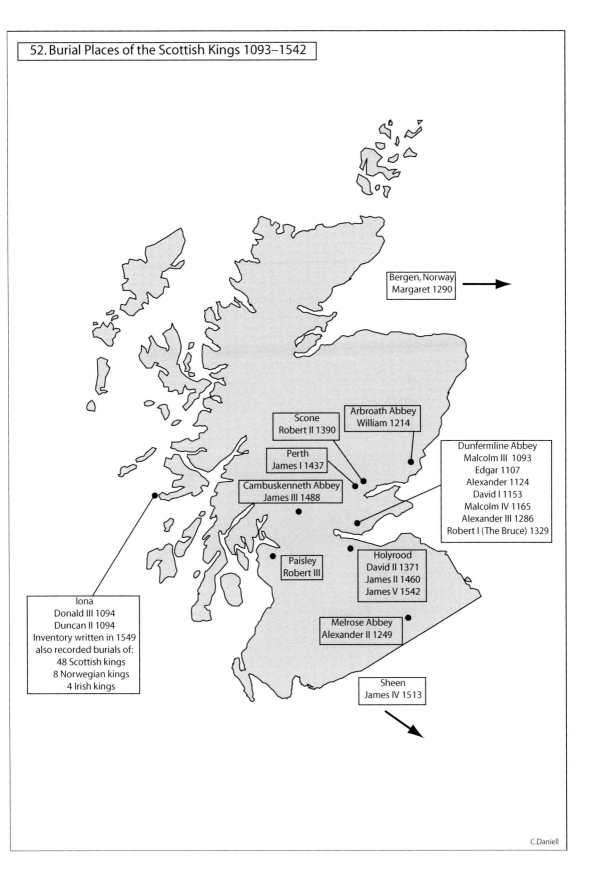

52. Burial Places of the Scottish Kings 1093–1542

Bergen, Norway
Margaret 1290

Scone
Robert II 1390

Arbroath Abbey
William 1214

Perth
James I 1437

Dunfermline Abbey
Malcolm III 1093
Edgar 1107
Alexander 1124
David I 1153
Malcolm IV 1165
Alexander III 1286
Robert I (The Bruce) 1329

Cambuskenneth Abbey
James III 1488

Paisley
Robert III

Holyrood
David II 1371
James II 1460
James V 1542

Iona
Donald III 1094
Duncan II 1094
Inventory written in 1549
also recorded burials of:
48 Scottish kings
8 Norwegian kings
4 Irish kings

Melrose Abbey
Alexander II 1249

Sheen
James IV 1513

C.Daniell

59

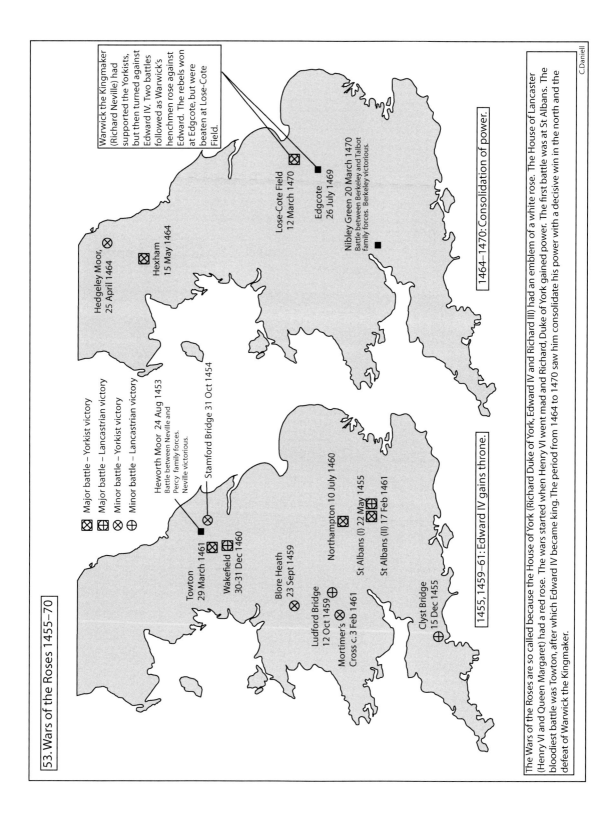

53. Wars of the Roses 1455–70

⊠ Major battle – Yorkist victory
⊞ Major battle – Lancastrian victory
⊗ Minor battle – Yorkist victory
⊕ Minor battle – Lancastrian victory

Wars of the Roses 1455–70

Heworth Moor 24 Aug 1453
Battle between Neville and Percy family forces. Neville victorious.

Stamford Bridge 31 Oct 1454

Towton 29 March 1461
Wakefield 30-31 Dec 1460
Blore Heath 23 Sept 1459
Ludford Bridge 12 Oct 1459
Mortimer's Cross c. 3 Feb 1461
Northampton 10 July 1460
St Albans (I) 22 May 1455
St Albans (II) 17 Feb 1461
Clyst Bridge 15 Dec 1455

1455, 1459–61: Edward IV gains throne.

Hedgeley Moor, 25 April 1464
Hexham 15 May 1464

Warwick the Kingmaker (Richard Neville) had supported the Yorkists, but then turned against Edward IV. Two battles followed as Warwick's henchmen rose against Edward. The rebels won at Edgcote, but were beaten at Lose-Cote Field.

Lose-Cote Field 12 March 1470
Edgcote 26 July 1469
Nibley Green 20 March 1470
Battle between Berkeley and Talbot family forces. Berkeley victorious.

1464–1470: Consolidation of power.

The Wars of the Roses are so called because the House of York (Richard Duke of York, Edward IV and Richard III) had an emblem of a white rose. The House of Lancaster (Henry VI and Queen Margaret) had a red rose. The wars started when Henry VI went mad and Richard, Duke of York gained power. The first battle was at St Albans. The bloodiest battle was Towton, after which Edward IV became king. The period from 1464 to 1470 saw him consolidate his power with a decisive win in the north and the defeat of Warwick the Kingmaker.

C.Daniell

60

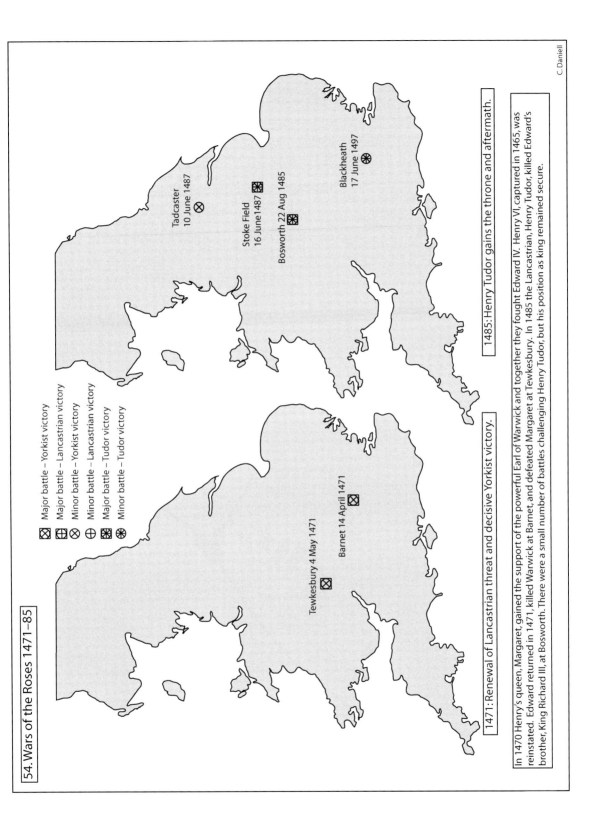

54. Wars of the Roses 1471–85

Major battle – Yorkist victory
Major battle – Lancastrian victory
Minor battle – Yorkist victory
Minor battle – Lancastrian victory
Major battle – Tudor victory
Minor battle – Tudor victory

Tadcaster
10 June 1487

Stoke Field
16 June 1487

Bosworth 22 Aug 1485

Blackheath
17 June 1497

Tewkesbury 4 May 1471

Barnet 14 April 1471

1471: Renewal of Lancastrian threat and decisive Yorkist victory.

1485: Henry Tudor gains the throne and aftermath.

In 1470 Henry's queen, Margaret, gained the support of the powerful Earl of Warwick and together they fought Edward IV. Henry VI, captured in 1465, was reinstated. Edward returned in 1471, killed Warwick at Barnet, and defeated Margaret at Tewkesbury. In 1485 the Lancastrian, Henry Tudor, killed Edward's brother, King Richard III, at Bosworth. There were a small number of battles challenging Henry Tudor, but his position as king remained secure.

C. Daniell

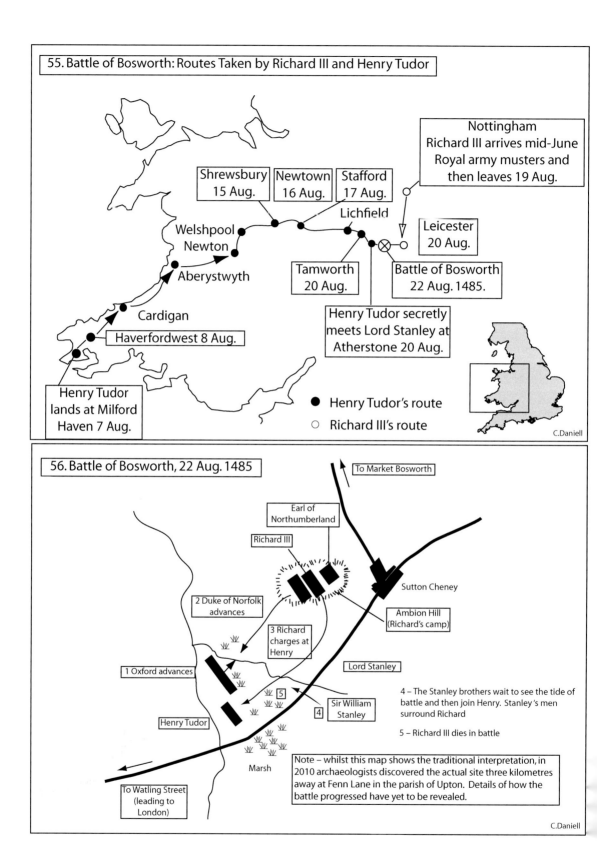

55. Battle of Bosworth: Routes Taken by Richard III and Henry Tudor

56. Battle of Bosworth, 22 Aug. 1485

GOVERNMENT, SOCIETY AND ECONOMY

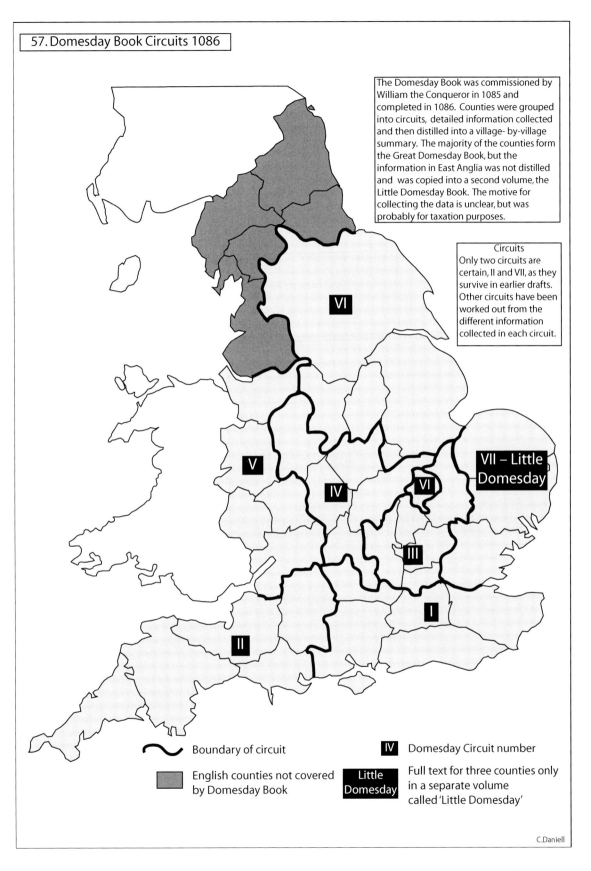

57. Domesday Book Circuits 1086

The Domesday Book was commissioned by William the Conqueror in 1085 and completed in 1086. Counties were grouped into circuits, detailed information collected and then distilled into a village- by-village summary. The majority of the counties form the Great Domesday Book, but the information in East Anglia was not distilled and was copied into a second volume, the Little Domesday Book. The motive for collecting the data is unclear, but was probably for taxation purposes.

Circuits
Only two circuits are certain, II and VII, as they survive in earlier drafts. Other circuits have been worked out from the different information collected in each circuit.

VI

V

IV

VI

VII – Little Domesday

III

I

II

∿ Boundary of circuit

IV Domesday Circuit number

English counties not covered by Domesday Book

Little Domesday Full text for three counties only in a separate volume called 'Little Domesday'

C.Daniell

65

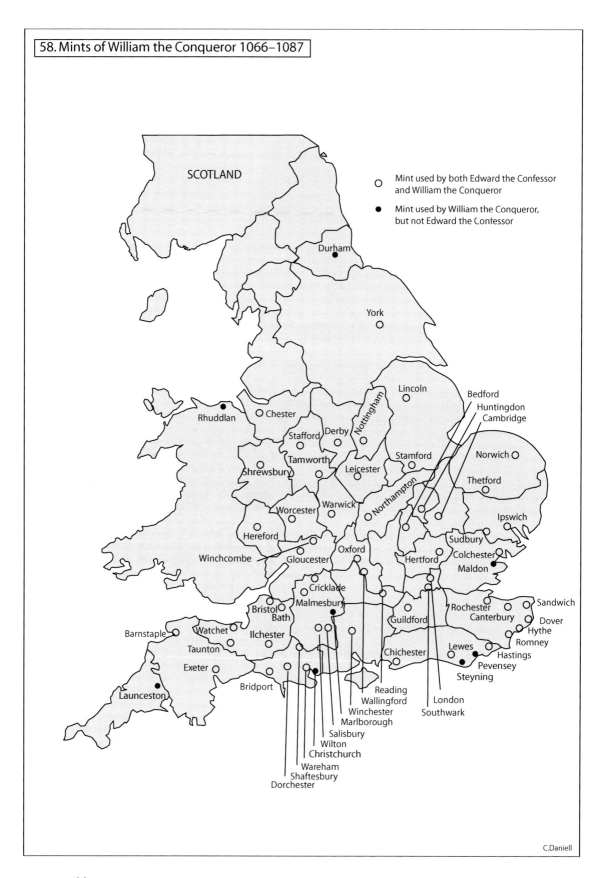

58. Mints of William the Conqueror 1066–1087

SCOTLAND

○ Mint used by both Edward the Confessor and William the Conqueror

● Mint used by William the Conqueror, but not Edward the Confessor

Durham

York

Lincoln

Bedford
Huntingdon
Cambridge

Rhuddlan   Chester

Stafford   Derby   Nottingham

Norwich

Tamworth   Stamford

Shrewsbury   Leicester   Thetford

Worcester   Warwick   Northampton   Ipswich

Hereford   Sudbury

Winchcombe   Oxford   Hertford   Colchester
Gloucester   Maldon

Cricklade

Bristol   Malmesbury   Rochester   Sandwich
Bath   Canterbury   Dover
Barnstaple   Watchet   Guildford   Hythe
Taunton   Ilchester   Romney
Exeter   Chichester   Lewes   Hastings
Bridport   Pevensey
Launceston   Steyning

Reading   London
Wallingford   Southwark
Winchester
Marlborough
Salisbury
Wilton
Christchurch
Wareham
Shaftesbury
Dorchester

C.Daniell

66

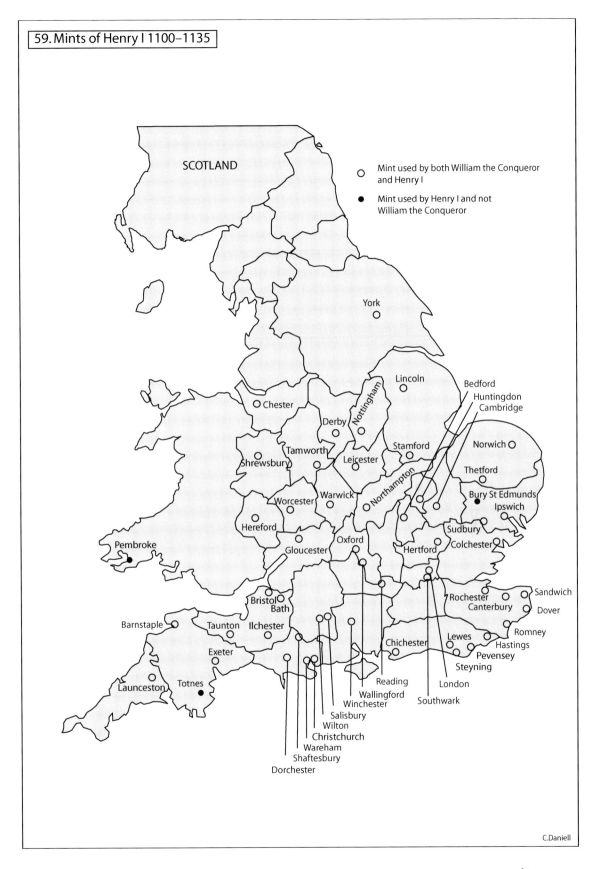

59. Mints of Henry I 1100–1135

SCOTLAND

○ Mint used by both William the Conqueror and Henry I

● Mint used by Henry I and not William the Conqueror

York

Lincoln

Bedford
Huntingdon
Cambridge

Chester

Nottingham

Derby

Stamford

Norwich

Tamworth

Shrewsbury

Leicester

Thetford

Worcester

Warwick

Northampton

Bury St Edmunds
Ipswich

Hereford

Oxford

Sudbury

Gloucester

Hertford

Colchester

Pembroke

Bristol
Bath

Rochester

Sandwich

Canterbury

Dover

Barnstaple

Taunton

Ilchester

Chichester

Lewes

Romney

Hastings

Exeter

Pevensey

Steyning

Launceston

Totnes

Reading

London

Wallingford

Southwark

Winchester

Salisbury

Wilton

Christchurch

Wareham

Shaftesbury

Dorchester

C.Daniell

67

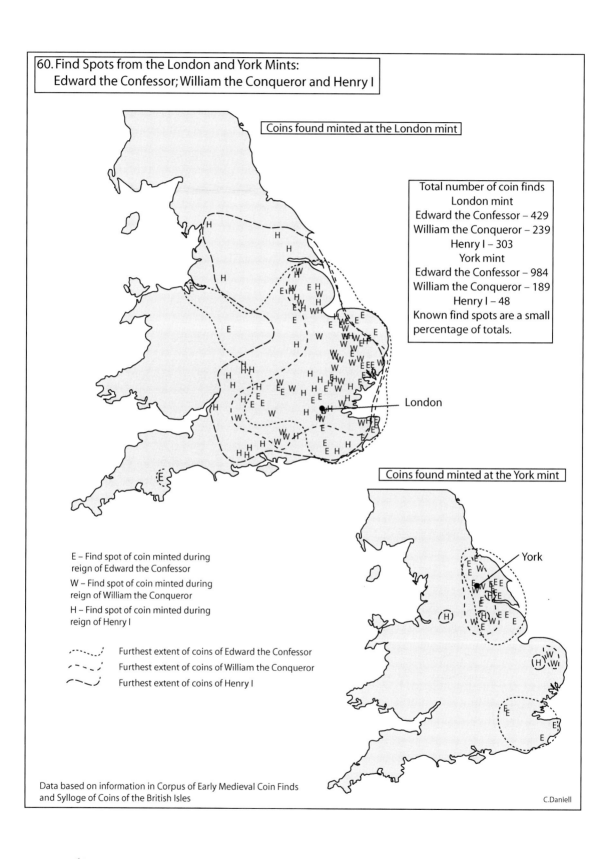

60. Find Spots from the London and York Mints:
Edward the Confessor; William the Conqueror and Henry I

Coins found minted at the London mint

Total number of coin finds
London mint
Edward the Confessor – 429
William the Conqueror – 239
Henry I – 303
York mint
Edward the Confessor – 984
William the Conqueror – 189
Henry I – 48
Known find spots are a small
percentage of totals.

London

Coins found minted at the York mint

York

E – Find spot of coin minted during
reign of Edward the Confessor

W – Find spot of coin minted during
reign of William the Conqueror

H – Find spot of coin minted during
reign of Henry I

....../ Furthest extent of coins of Edward the Confessor

- - -./ Furthest extent of coins of William the Conqueror

~ - -./ Furthest extent of coins of Henry I

Data based on information in Corpus of Early Medieval Coin Finds
and Sylloge of Coins of the British Isles

C.Daniell

68

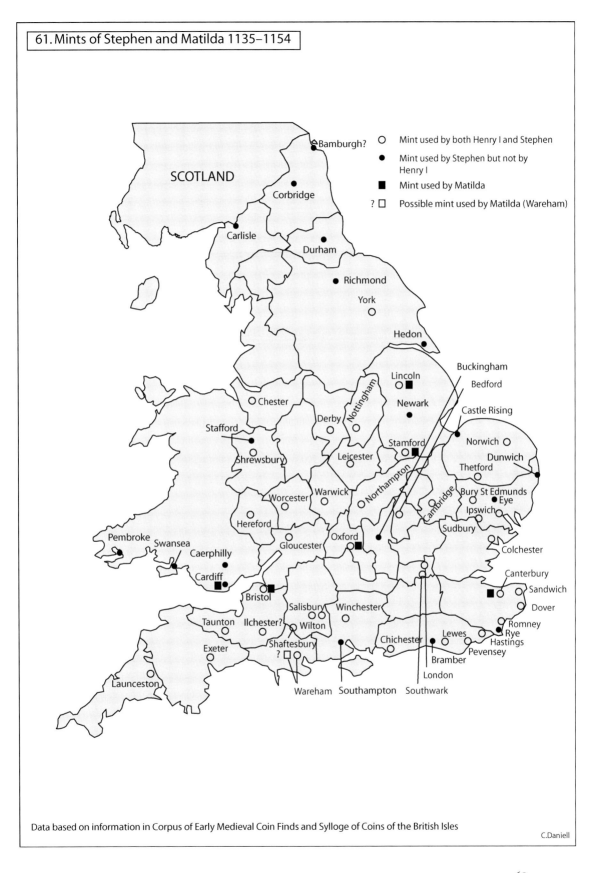

61. Mints of Stephen and Matilda 1135–1154

SCOTLAND

Bamburgh?

Corbridge

Carlisle

Durham

Richmond

York

Hedon

Buckingham

Bedford

Lincoln

Newark

Castle Rising

Chester

Derby

Stafford

Nottingham

Shrewsbury

Leicester

Stamford

Norwich

Dunwich

Thetford

Warwick

Northampton

Worcester

Cambridge

Bury St Edmunds

Hereford

Ipswich

Eye

Pembroke

Swansea

Gloucester

Oxford

Sudbury

Caerphilly

Colchester

Cardiff

Canterbury

Bristol

Salisbury

Winchester

Sandwich

Taunton

Ilchester?

Wilton

Dover

Chichester

Lewes

Romney

Exeter

Shaftesbury

Bramber

Rye

Hastings

Pevensey

?

Launceston

Wareham Southampton Southwark

London

○ Mint used by both Henry I and Stephen

● Mint used by Stephen but not by Henry I

■ Mint used by Matilda

? □ Possible mint used by Matilda (Wareham)

Data based on information in Corpus of Early Medieval Coin Finds and Sylloge of Coins of the British Isles

C.Daniell

69

SCOTLAND

Carlisle

Durham

York

Lincoln

Norwich

Shrewsbury

Warwick

Northampton

Bury St Edmunds

Hereford

Oxford

Gloucester

London

Wallingford

Bristol

Wilton

Winchester

Canterbury

Ilchester

Exeter

Data based on information in Corpus of Early Medieval Coin Finds and Sylloge of Coins of the British Isles

C.Daniell

The number and operation of each mint varied considerably depending on the power and influence of the king. The evidence for mints at Chester and Inverness come from single coins and at Dumfries from three coins, all in the reign of Alexander III (1249–86).

Inverness ● A

Aberdeen ●
A

Montrose
Forfar ● A ●
A

D Perth
W A St Andrews
A ●

Stirling
● A Kinghorn A

A Renfrew
●
A Glasgow
Edinburgh A
●
Lanark A
●

Berwick
A D ●

Roxburgh ●
D W A

Ayr ●
A

Dumfries ?
A

D Carlisle

Chester
A

D Mints of King David 1124–53

W Mints of King William 1165–1214

A Mints of King Alexander III 1249–86

Two other kings had mints – one coin is known from an unknown mint of Malcolm IV (1153–65), and Alexander II (1214–49) had a mint at Roxburgh.·

Find locations of Scottish coins in England

Data based on information in Corpus of Early Medieval Coin Finds and Sylloge of Coins of the British Isles

C.Daniell

71

SCOTLAND

Newcastle

Carlisle

Durham

York

Beverley

Lincoln

Chester

Nottingham

Leicester

Norwich

Shrewsbury

Warwick

Yarmouth

Worcester

Hereford

Northampton

Oxford

St Albans

Canterbury

Bristol

London

Salisbury

Winchester

Dover

Exeter

- - - - Road

Navigable River

● Important town on nodal point

By permission of P. Hindle, *Medieval Tracks and Roads, No 26 Shire Archaeology*, Shire Publications Ltd 1998, p. 59

C. Daniell

65. Road Networks as Used by King John, Edward I and Edward II

A   Abingdon
C   Canterbury
F   Freemantle
K   Kings Langley
KC   King's Cliffe
L   London
LB   Leighton Buzzard
M   Marlborough
O   Oxford
Od   Odiham
R   Reading
S   Southampton
SA   St Albans
T   Tewkesbury
W   Windsor
Wa   Wallingford
Wi   Winchester
Wo   Woodstock

Berwick

Newcastle

Darlington
Northallerton

York   Beverley

Pontefract
Doncaster

Walsingham

Nottingham

Shrewsbury

Leicester   Norwich
                   Stamford
                   KC   Ely   Thetford
Ludlow   Bury
                   Northampton   St Edmunds
Hereford   Towcester   Newmarket

Gloucester   T   Brill   LB
                   Wo   O   K   SA   Ware
                   A   Wa   Rochester
                        R   W   Leeds
Bristol   M   Od   L   C
                   F   Dover
Salisbury   Wi   Guildford
                   S   Farnham
Dorchester

Ringwood

By permission of P. Hindle, *Medieval Tracks and Roads, No 26 Shire Archaeology*, Shire Publications Ltd, 1998, p. 28   C.Daniell

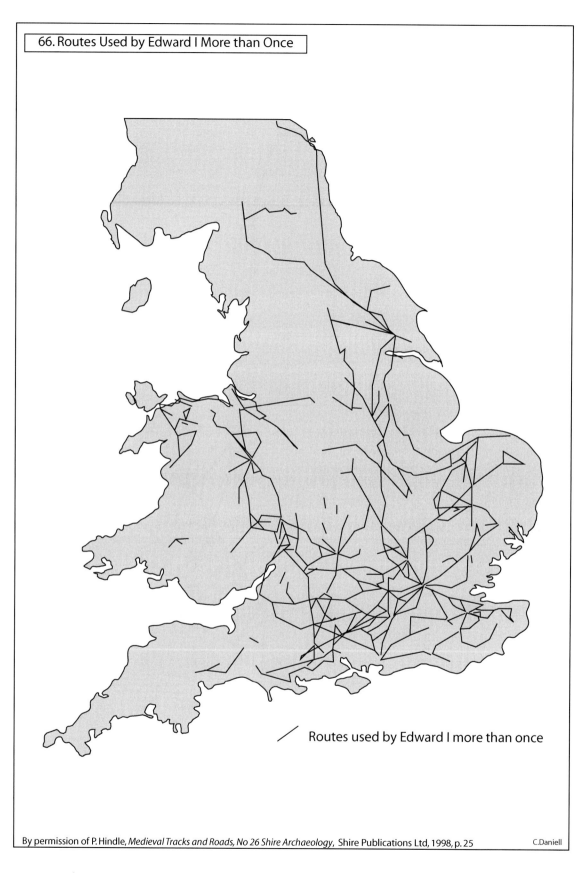

66. Routes Used by Edward I More than Once

Routes used by Edward I more than once

By permission of P. Hindle, *Medieval Tracks and Roads, No 26 Shire Archaeology*, Shire Publications Ltd, 1998, p. 25

C.Daniell

Lynn 5
Yarmouth 3
Dunwich 5/2
Ipswich 2
Ireland 5/6
Gloucester 1
Thames at 'Newebree' 0/2
Sandwich 4/3
Bristol 3/2
London 5
Portsmouth 0/4
Southampton 2/1
Romney 4/3
Rye 3
Winchelsea 2/2
Exeter 2
Newhaven 2
Shoreham 5/2

Key:
Name of port   Number of ships in 1235
Shoreham 5/2
Number of ships in 1206
(single number = 1206)

Medieval kings required ports to have available a certain number of ships for naval duties or war. Most of the ships were merchant ships, and whilst the navy lists are not a complete inventory of all ships, they give a good idea of the importance of ports and distribution of ships. Detailed lists survive from the 14th century and show huge variation in the requirements for up to 180 ports per year.

C.Daniell

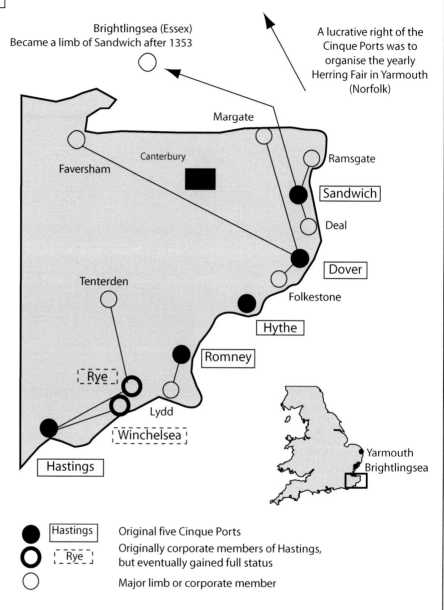

68. Cinque Ports

Brightlingsea (Essex)
Became a limb of Sandwich after 1353

A lucrative right of the Cinque Ports was to organise the yearly Herring Fair in Yarmouth (Norfolk)

Margate

Canterbury

Faversham

Ramsgate

Sandwich

Deal

Dover

Tenterden

Folkestone

Hythe

Romney

Rye

Lydd

Winchelsea

Hastings

Yarmouth
Brightlingsea

● Hastings — Original five Cinque Ports

◯ Rye — Originally corporate members of Hastings, but eventually gained full status

○ — Major limb or corporate member

The Cinque Ports (pronounced 'sink') originally comprised five ports (Hastings, Romney, Hythe, Dover and Sandwich). The ports were required to supply 57 ships for 15 days every year, either for warfare or transport for the ruler and his entourage. In return the ports were granted their own rights, such as levying local taxes. A system developed whereby other towns or villages were 'limbs' to the original port and they helped the head port with their service and gained rights in return. Larger limb communities gained their own charters and so became 'corporate members' of the Ports.

C. Daniell

69. London's Wards and Wealth 1332

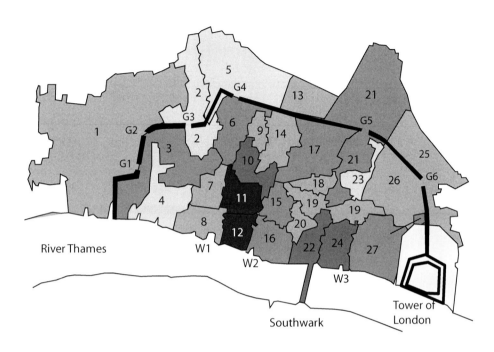

River Thames

Southwark

Tower of London

1 Farringdon Without
2 Aldersgate
3 Farringdon Within
4 Castle Baynard
5 Cripplegate Without
6 Cripplegate Within
7 Bread Street
8 Queenshithe
9 Bassishaw
10 Cheap
11 Cordwainer
12 Vintry
13 Coleman Street
14 Coleman Street
15 Walbrook
16 Dowgate (Downgate)
17 Broad Street
18 Cornhill
19 Langbourn
20 Candlewick
21 Bishopsgate
22 Bridge
23 Lime Street
24 Billingsgate
25 Portsoken
26 Aldgate
27 Tower

Gates

G1 Ludgate
G2 Newgate
G3 Aldersgate
G4 Cripplegate
G5 Bishopsgate
G6 Aldgate

Important Medieval Wharfs

W1 Queenshithe Wharf
W2 Hanseatic Steelyard Wharf
W3 Billingsgate Wharf

Mean tax paid
per tax payer,
based on 1332
Lay Subsidy

Over 10 shillings (s)

6s–7s

4s–6s

2s–4s

Less than 2s

C.Daniell

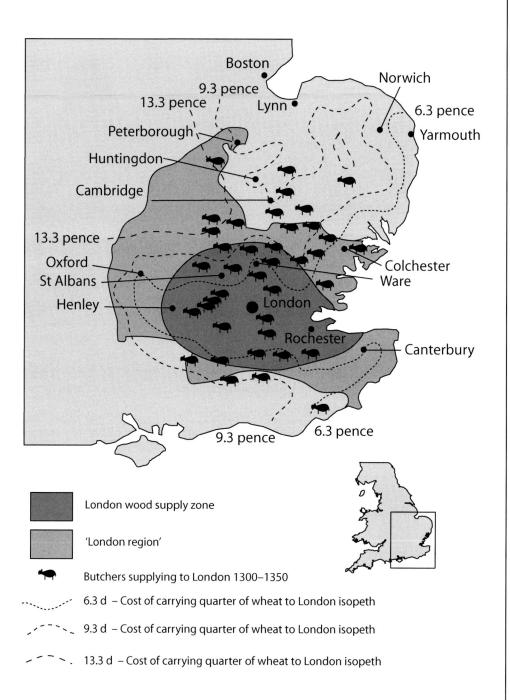

Boston
9.3 pence
13.3 pence
Lynn
Norwich
6.3 pence
Yarmouth
Peterborough
Huntingdon
Cambridge
13.3 pence
Oxford
St Albans
Henley
London
Colchester
Ware
Rochester
Canterbury
9.3 pence
6.3 pence

London wood supply zone

'London region'

Butchers supplying to London 1300–1350

6.3 d – Cost of carrying quarter of wheat to London isopeth

9.3 d – Cost of carrying quarter of wheat to London isopeth

13.3 d – Cost of carrying quarter of wheat to London isopeth

C.Daniell

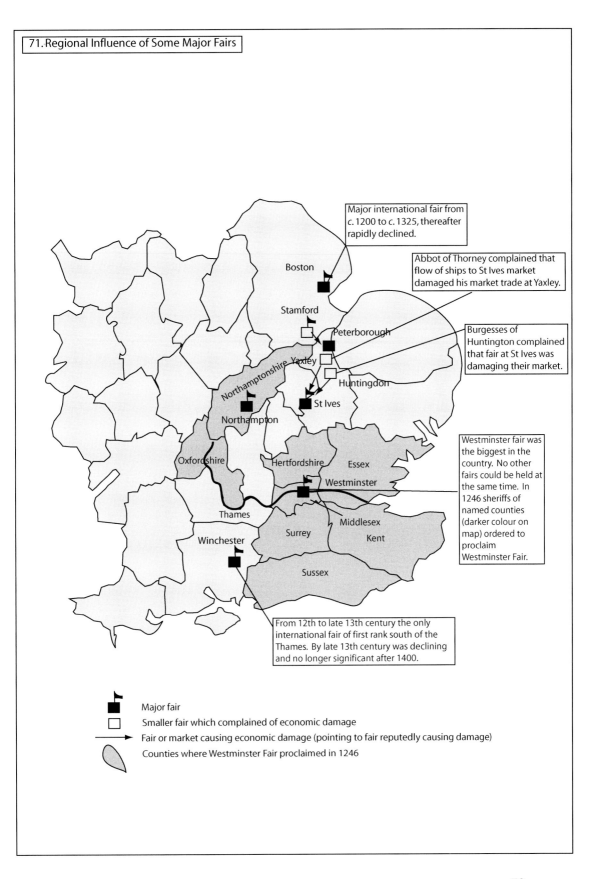

Boston

Major international fair from *c.* 1200 to *c.* 1325, thereafter rapidly declined.

Stamford

Peterborough

Abbot of Thorney complained that flow of ships to St Ives market damaged his market trade at Yaxley.

Yaxley

Huntingdon

Burgesses of Huntington complained that fair at St Ives was damaging their market.

Northamptonshire

St Ives

Northampton

Oxfordshire

Hertfordshire

Essex

Westminster

Westminster fair was the biggest in the country. No other fairs could be held at the same time. In 1246 sheriffs of named counties (darker colour on map) ordered to proclaim Westminster Fair.

Thames

Middlesex

Surrey

Kent

Winchester

Sussex

From 12th to late 13th century the only international fair of first rank south of the Thames. By late 13th century was declining and no longer significant after 1400.

■ Major fair
☐ Smaller fair which complained of economic damage
→ Fair or market causing economic damage (pointing to fair reputedly causing damage)
⬭ Counties where Westminster Fair proclaimed in 1246

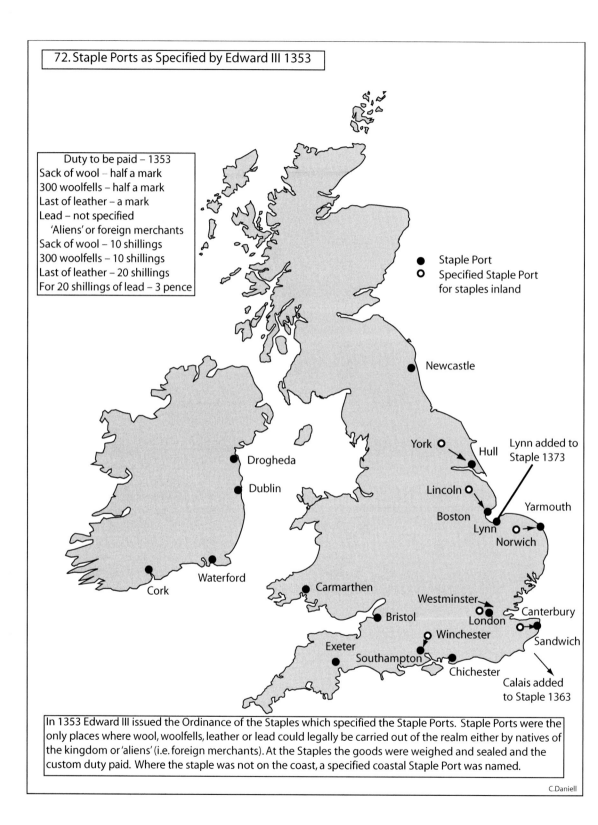

72. Staple Ports as Specified by Edward III 1353

Duty to be paid – 1353
Sack of wool – half a mark
300 woolfells – half a mark
Last of leather – a mark
Lead – not specified
'Aliens' or foreign merchants
Sack of wool – 10 shillings
300 woolfells – 10 shillings
Last of leather – 20 shillings
For 20 shillings of lead – 3 pence

● Staple Port
○ Specified Staple Port
for staples inland

Newcastle

York ○
Hull

Lynn added to
Staple 1373

Drogheda

Dublin

Lincoln ○

Boston

Yarmouth

Lynn
Norwich

Waterford

Cork

Carmarthen

Westminster

Canterbury

Bristol

London

Winchester

Sandwich

Exeter

Southampton

Chichester

Calais added
to Staple 1363

In 1353 Edward III issued the Ordinance of the Staples which specified the Staple Ports. Staple Ports were the only places where wool, woolfells, leather or lead could legally be carried out of the realm either by natives of the kingdom or 'aliens' (i.e. foreign merchants). At the Staples the goods were weighed and sealed and the custom duty paid. Where the staple was not on the coast, a specified coastal Staple Port was named.

C.Daniell

73. Late 14th Century English Cloth Industry

Approximate average annual production
of Broadcloths or equivalent by county

Over 10,000 cloths

5,000–10,000 cloths

1,000–5,000 cloths

Below 1,000 cloths

Information incomplete

● Centres producing over 1,000 cloths

York ●

Coventry ●

Hadleigh ●

London ●

Colchester ●

Bath

Bristol

Frome

Wells

Salisbury ●

Pensford

Winchester ●

Adapted from R.A. Pelham, 'Fourteenth-Century England', in H.C. Darby, *An Historical Geography of England before 1800*, CUP, 1969

C.Daniell

81

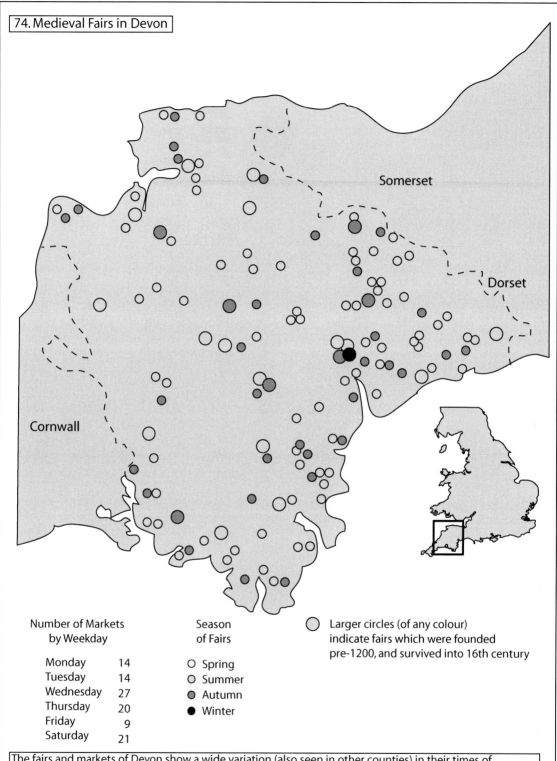

74. Medieval Fairs in Devon

Somerset

Dorset

Cornwall

Number of Markets by Weekday		Season of Fairs		Larger circles (of any colour) indicate fairs which were founded pre-1200, and survived into 16th century
Monday	14	○ Spring		
Tuesday	14	○ Summer		
Wednesday	27	◑ Autumn		
Thursday	20	● Winter		
Friday	9			
Saturday	21			

The fairs and markets of Devon show a wide variation (also seen in other counties) in their times of operation. Only a minority of fairs (the larger circles) lasted from pre-1200 to the 16th century, whilst approximately 50 per cent did not survive past 1350. Location of fairs only shown on the above map.

By permission of M. Kowaleski, *Local Markets and Regional Trade in Medieval Exeter*, Cambridge University Press, 1995   C.Daniell

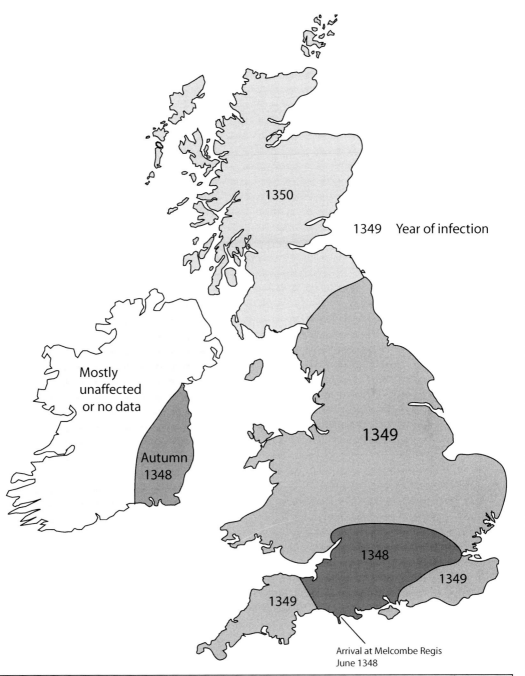

75. The Black Death 1348–1350

1350

1349   Year of infection

Mostly
unaffected
or no data

Autumn
1348

1349

1348

1349

1349

Arrival at Melcombe Regis
June 1348

The Black Death, or bubonic plague, had swept through Europe and arrived in England in the summer of 1348. By the end of the outbreak, an estimated third to half the population had died. The resulting social upheaval resulted in price rises and labour shortages. Further outbreaks, though not so devastating, occurred in 1361, 1369, 1379–83 and 1389–93, with recurrent outbreaks in the 15th century.

C.Daniell

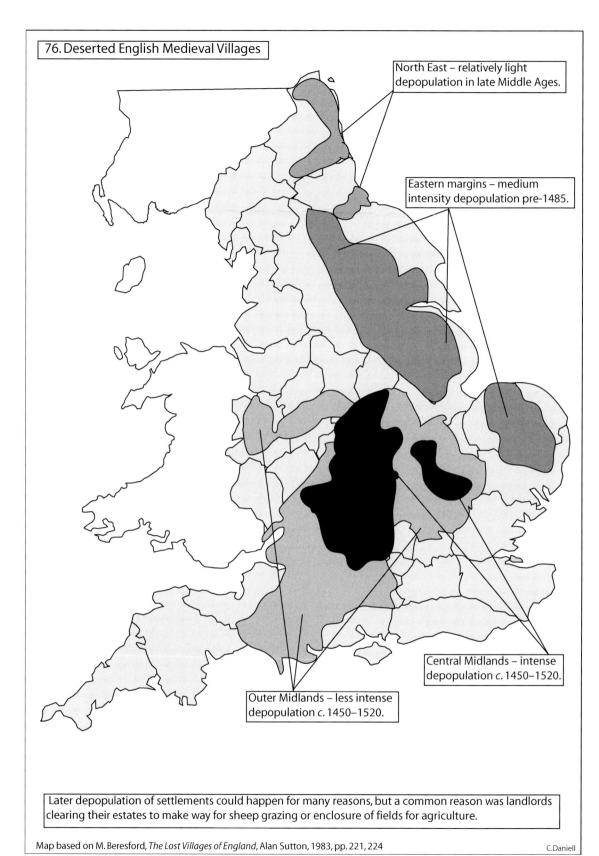

76. Deserted English Medieval Villages

North East – relatively light depopulation in late Middle Ages.

Eastern margins – medium intensity depopulation pre-1485.

Central Midlands – intense depopulation c. 1450–1520.

Outer Midlands – less intense depopulation c. 1450–1520.

Later depopulation of settlements could happen for many reasons, but a common reason was landlords clearing their estates to make way for sheep grazing or enclosure of fields for agriculture.

Map based on M. Beresford, *The Lost Villages of England*, Alan Sutton, 1983, pp. 221, 224

C. Daniell

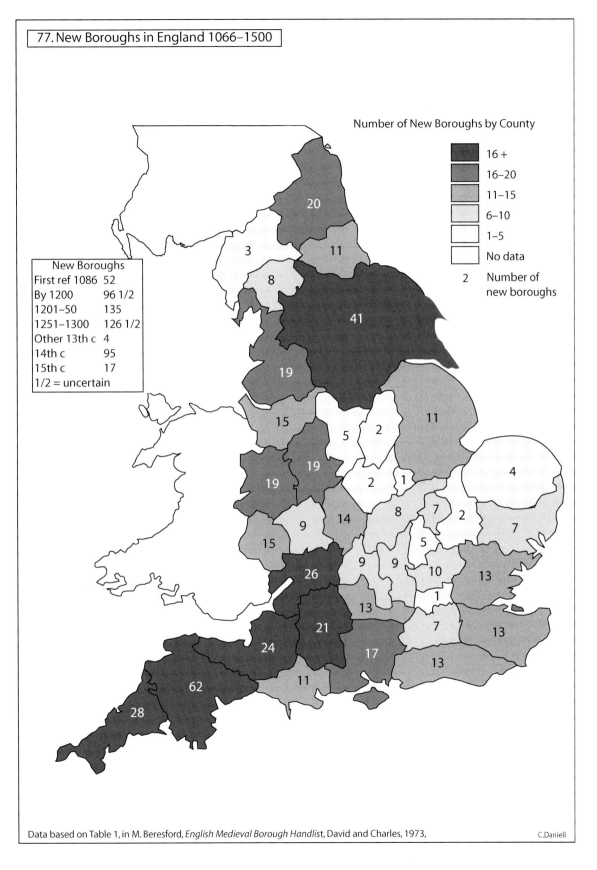

77. New Boroughs in England 1066–1500

Number of New Boroughs by County

- 16 +
- 16–20
- 11–15
- 6–10
- 1–5
- No data
- 2   Number of new boroughs

New Boroughs

First ref 1086	52
By 1200	96 1/2
1201–50	135
1251–1300	126 1/2
Other 13th c	4
14th c	95
15th c	17
1/2 = uncertain	

Map values:
20, 3, 11, 8, 41, 19, 11, 15, 5, 2, 19, 4, 19, 2, 1, 9, 14, 8, 7, 2, 7, 5, 15, 9, 9, 10, 13, 26, 1, 21, 13, 7, 13, 24, 17, 13, 11, 62, 28

Data based on Table 1, in M. Beresford, *English Medieval Borough Handlist*, David and Charles, 1973,

C.Daniell

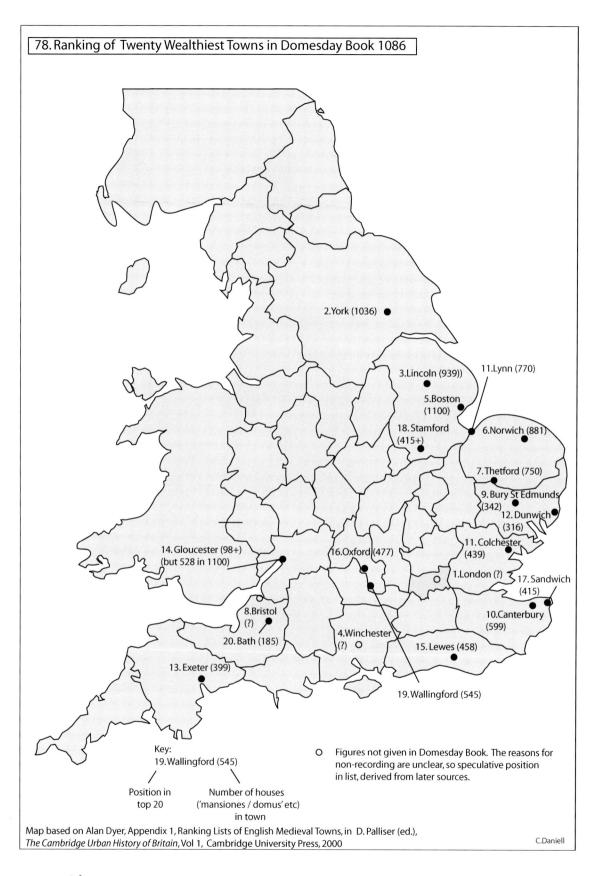

78. Ranking of Twenty Wealthiest Towns in Domesday Book 1086

2.York (1036) ●

3.Lincoln (939)) ●

11.Lynn (770)

5.Boston (1100) ●

18. Stamford (415+) ●

6.Norwich (881) ●

7.Thetford (750) ●

9. Bury St Edmunds (342) ●

12. Dunwich (316) ●

11. Colchester (439) ●

14. Gloucester (98+) (but 528 in 1100) ●

16.Oxford (477) ●

1.London (?) ○

17. Sandwich (415) ●

8.Bristol (?) ○

10.Canterbury (599) ●

20. Bath (185) ●

4.Winchester (?) ○

15. Lewes (458) ●

13. Exeter (399) ●

19. Wallingford (545)

Key:
19.Wallingford (545)

Position in top 20 / Number of houses ('mansiones / domus' etc) in town

○ Figures not given in Domesday Book. The reasons for non-recording are unclear, so speculative position in list, derived from later sources.

Map based on Alan Dyer, Appendix 1, Ranking Lists of English Medieval Towns, in D. Palliser (ed.), *The Cambridge Urban History of Britain*, Vol 1, Cambridge University Press, 2000

C.Daniell

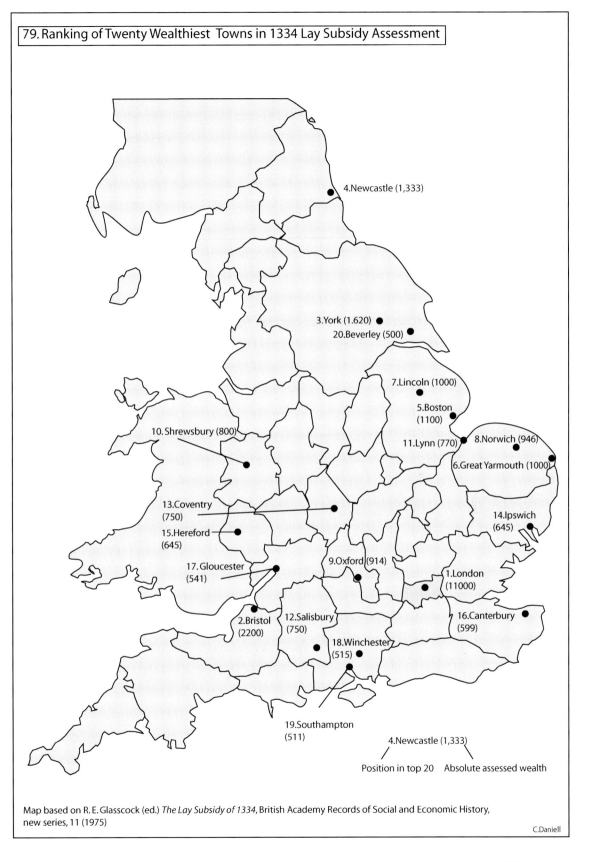

79. Ranking of Twenty Wealthiest Towns in 1334 Lay Subsidy Assessment

4.Newcastle (1,333)

3.York (1.620)
20.Beverley (500)

7.Lincoln (1000)

5.Boston (1100)

10. Shrewsbury (800)

11.Lynn (770)

8.Norwich (946)

6.Great Yarmouth (1000)

13.Coventry (750)

14.Ipswich (645)

15.Hereford (645)

17. Gloucester (541)

9.Oxford (914)

1.London (11000)

2.Bristol (2200)

12.Salisbury (750)

16.Canterbury (599)

18.Winchester (515)

19.Southampton (511)

4.Newcastle (1,333)

Position in top 20   Absolute assessed wealth

Map based on R. E. Glasscock (ed.) *The Lay Subsidy of 1334*, British Academy Records of Social and Economic History, new series, 11 (1975)

C.Daniell

87

80. Ranking of Twenty Wealthiest Towns by 1377 Poll Tax Assessment

12.Newcastle (2,647)

2.York (7,248)
11.Beverley (2,663)

6.Lincoln (3,569)
10.Boston (2,871)

5.Norwich (3,952)

20. Shrewsbury (1.932)

8. Lynn (3,127)

19.Yarmouth (1,941)

17.Leicester (2,302)

4.Coventry (4,817)

15.Bury St Edmunds (2,445)

9. Colchester (2,951)

18. Gloucester (2239)

16.Oxford (2,357)

1.London (23,314)

3.Bristol (6,345)

7.Salisbury (3,373)

13.Canterbury (2,574)

14.Winchester (2,500?)

7. Salisbury (3,373)

Position in top 20   Number of recorded taxpayers

Map based on Alan Dyer, Appendix 1, Ranking Lists of English Medieval Towns, in D. Palliser (ed.), *The Cambridge Urban History of Britain*, Vol 1, Cambridge University Press, 2000

C.Daniell

RELIGION AND CULTURE

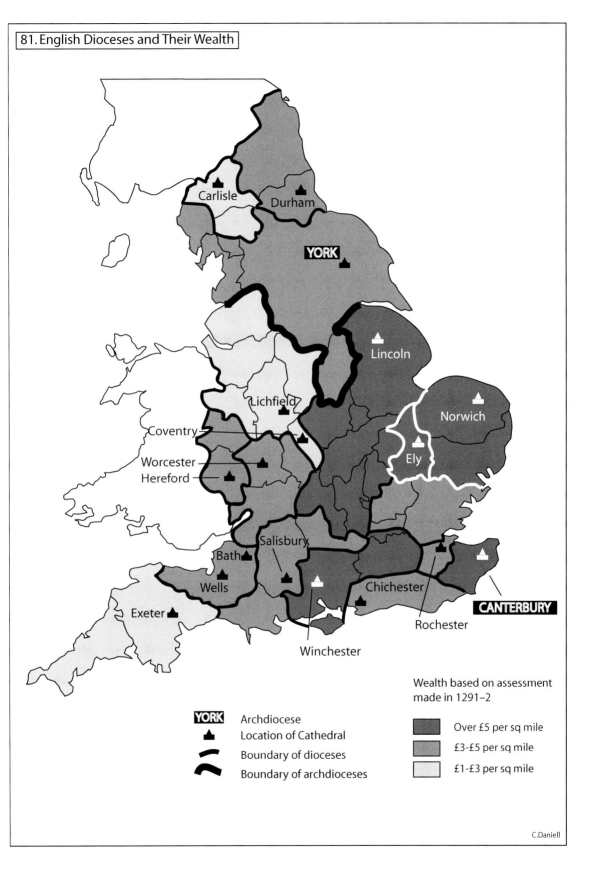

81. English Dioceses and Their Wealth

Carlisle
Durham
YORK
Lincoln
Norwich
Lichfield
Coventry
Worcester
Hereford
Ely
Salisbury
Bath
Wells
Chichester
CANTERBURY
Exeter
Rochester
Winchester

Wealth based on assessment
made in 1291–2

YORK — Archdiocese
▲ — Location of Cathedral
≈ — Boundary of dioceses
≈ — Boundary of archdioceses

Over £5 per sq mile
£3–£5 per sq mile
£1–£3 per sq mile

C.Daniell

91

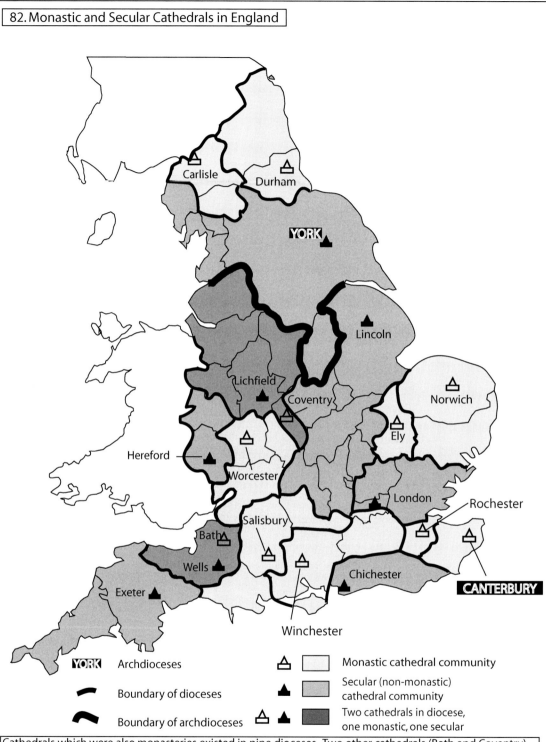

82. Monastic and Secular Cathedrals in England

Carlisle
Durham
YORK
Lincoln
Lichfield
Coventry
Norwich
Ely
Hereford
Worcester
London
Rochester
Salisbury
Bath
Wells
Chichester
CANTERBURY
Exeter
Winchester

YORK Archdioceses

Boundary of dioceses

Boundary of archdioceses

Monastic cathedral community

Secular (non-monastic) cathedral community

Two cathedrals in diocese, one monastic, one secular

Cathedrals which were also monasteries existed in nine dioceses. Two other cathedrals (Bath and Coventry) were monastic, and were joined by two secular cathedrals (Wells and Lichfield). Whilst monastic cathedrals were common in England, elsewhere in Europe such an arrangement was very rare. The bishop took the place of the abbot and ruled both the cathedral monastery and the diocese. Cathedral monasteries were first created in the Anglo-Saxon period and then spread after the Conquest.

C. Daniell

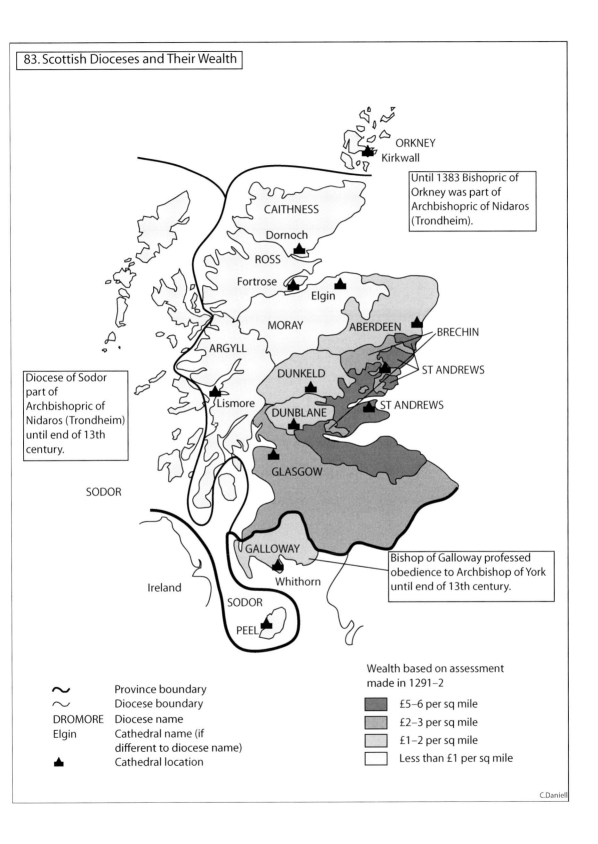

83. Scottish Dioceses and Their Wealth

ORKNEY
Kirkwall

Until 1383 Bishopric of Orkney was part of Archbishopric of Nidaros (Trondheim).

CAITHNESS

Dornoch

ROSS

Fortrose

Elgin

MORAY

ABERDEEN

BRECHIN

ARGYLL

St ANDREWS

Diocese of Sodor part of Archbishopric of Nidaros (Trondheim) until end of 13th century.

DUNKELD

Lismore

ST ANDREWS

DUNBLANE

GLASGOW

SODOR

GALLOWAY

Bishop of Galloway professed obedience to Archbishop of York until end of 13th century.

Ireland

Whithorn

SODOR

PEEL

Wealth based on assessment made in 1291–2

~ Province boundary
~ Diocese boundary
DROMORE Diocese name
Elgin Cathedral name (if different to diocese name)
▲ Cathedral location

£5–6 per sq mile
£2–3 per sq mile
£1–2 per sq mile
Less than £1 per sq mile

C.Daniell

93

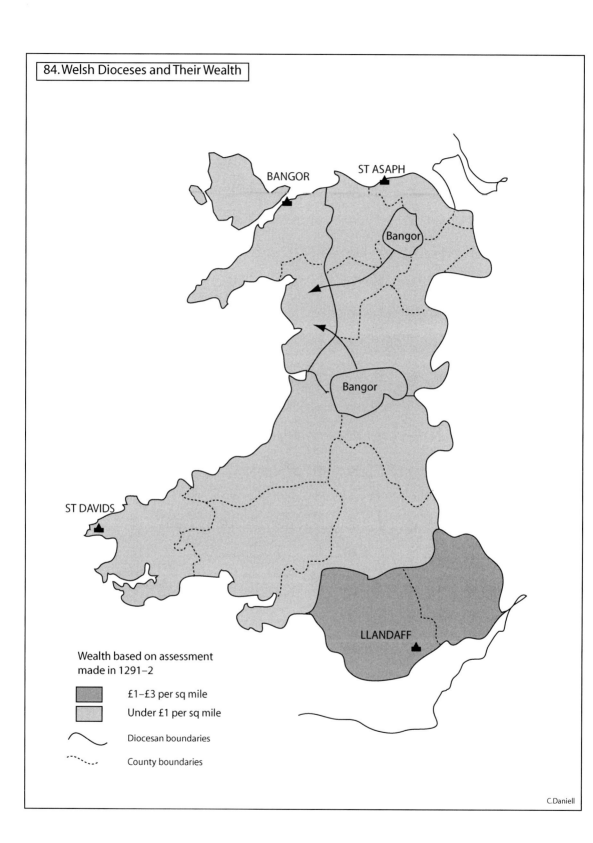

84. Welsh Dioceses and Their Wealth

BANGOR

ST ASAPH

Bangor

Bangor

ST DAVIDS

LLANDAFF

Wealth based on assessment
made in 1291–2

£1–£3 per sq mile

Under £1 per sq mile

Diocesan boundaries

County boundaries

C.Daniell

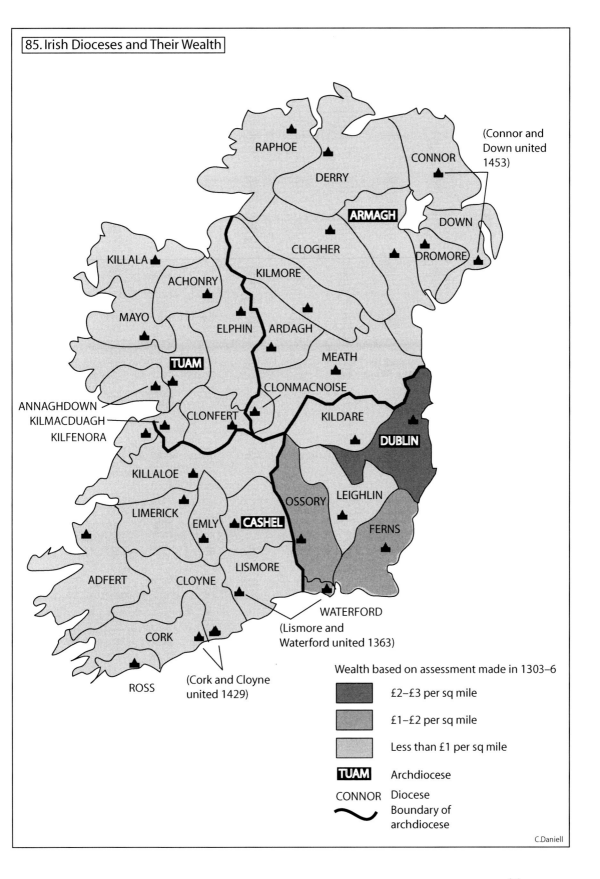

85. Irish Dioceses and Their Wealth

RAPHOE

DERRY

CONNOR

(Connor and Down united 1453)

ARMAGH

DOWN

CLOGHER

KILLALA

ACHONRY

KILMORE

DROMORE

MAYO

ELPHIN

ARDAGH

TUAM

MEATH

ANNAGHDOWN
KILMACDUAGH
KILFENORA

CLONMACNOISE

CLONFERT

KILDARE

DUBLIN

KILLALOE

LEIGHLIN

LIMERICK

OSSORY

FERNS

EMLY

CASHEL

ADFERT

LISMORE

CLOYNE

WATERFORD

(Lismore and
Waterford united 1363)

CORK

ROSS

(Cork and Cloyne
united 1429)

Wealth based on assessment made in 1303–6

£2–£3 per sq mile

£1–£2 per sq mile

Less than £1 per sq mile

TUAM Archdiocese

CONNOR Diocese

Boundary of archdiocese

C.Daniell

95

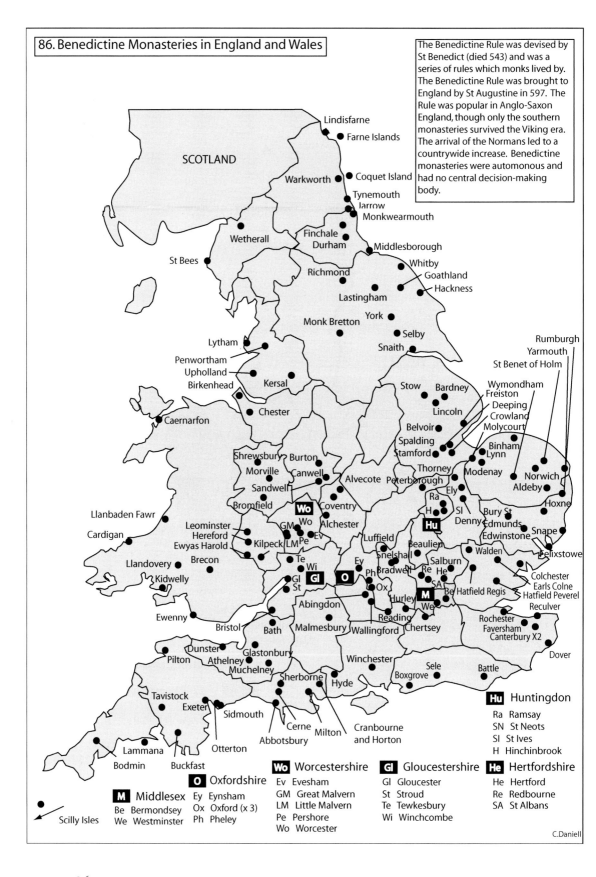

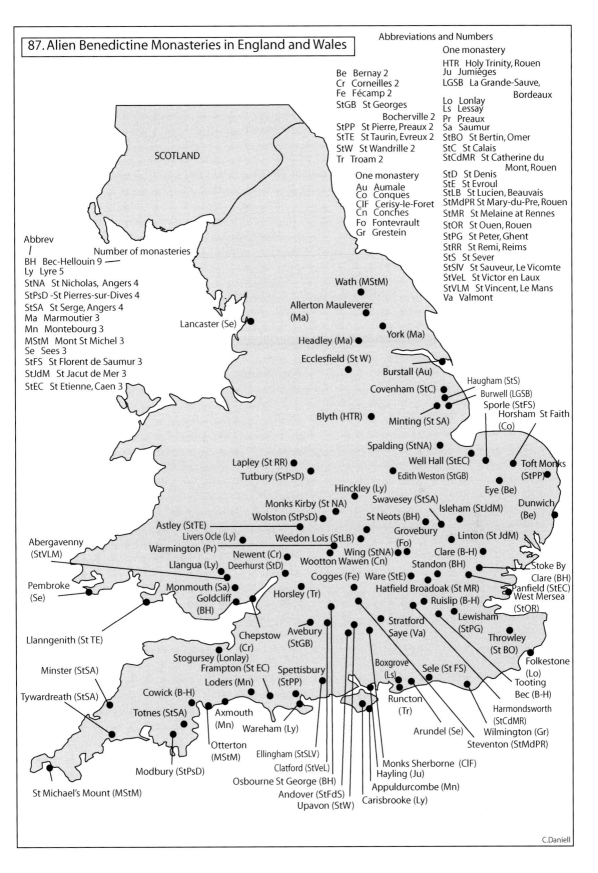

87. Alien Benedictine Monasteries in England and Wales

Abbreviations and Numbers

One monastery
- HTR Holy Trinity, Rouen
- Ju Jumièges
- LGSB La Grande-Sauve, Bordeaux

Two monasteries
- Be Bernay 2
- Cr Corneilles 2
- Fe Fécamp 2
- StGB St Georges Bocherville 2
- StPP St Pierre, Preaux 2
- StTE St Taurin, Evreux 2
- StW St Wandrille 2
- Tr Troam 2

One monastery
- Au Aumale
- Co Conques
- ClF Cerisy-le-Foret
- Cn Conches
- Fo Fontevrault
- Gr Grestein

One monastery
- Lo Lonlay
- Ls Lessay
- Pr Preaux
- Sa Saumur
- StBO St Bertin, Omer
- StC St Calais
- StCdMR St Catherine du Mont, Rouen
- StD St Denis
- StE St Evroul
- StLB St Lucien, Beauvais
- StMdPR St Mary-du-Pre, Rouen
- StMR St Melaine at Rennes
- StOR St Ouen, Rouen
- StPG St Peter, Ghent
- StRR St Remi, Reims
- StS St Sever
- StSlV St Sauveur, Le Vicomte
- StVeL St Victor en Laux
- StVLM St Vincent, Le Mans
- Va Valmont

Abbrev / Number of monasteries
- BH Bec-Helloin 9
- Ly Lyre 5
- StNA St Nicholas, Angers 4
- StPsD St Pierres-sur-Dives 4
- StSA St Serge, Angers 4
- Ma Marmoutier 3
- Mn Montebourg 3
- MStM Mont St Michel 3
- Se Sees 3
- StFS St Florent de Saumur 3
- StJdM St Jacut de Mer 3
- StEC St Etienne, Caen 3

SCOTLAND

Wath (MStM)

Allerton Mauleverer (Ma)

Lancaster (Se)

Headley (Ma)

York (Ma)

Ecclesfield (St W)

Burstall (Au)

Covenham (StC)

Haugham (StS)

Burwell (LGSB)

Sporle (StFS)

Horsham St Faith (Co)

Blyth (HTR)

Minting (St SA)

Spalding (StNA)

Well Hall (StEC)

Toft Monks (StPP)

Lapley (St RR)

Tutbury (StPsD)

Edith Weston (StGB)

Eye (Be)

Hinckley (Ly)

Swavesey (StSA)

Isleham (StJdM)

Dunwich (Be)

Monks Kirby (St NA)

Wolston (StPsD)

St Neots (BH)

Groebury (Fo)

Linton (St JdM)

Astley (StTE)

Livers Ocle (Ly)

Weedon Lois (StLB)

Clare (B-H)

Abergavenny (StVLM)

Warmington (Pr)

Newent (Cr)

Wing (StNA)

Clare (B-H)

Stoke By Clare (BH)

Llangua (Ly)

Deerhurst (StD)

Wootton Wawen (Cn)

Standon (BH)

Panfield (StEC)

Pembroke (Se)

Monmouth (Sa)

Cogges (Fe)

Ware (StE)

Hatfield Broadoak (St MR)

West Mersea (StOR)

Goldcliff (BH)

Horsley (Tr)

Ruislip (B-H)

Llanngenith (St TE)

Chepstow (Cr)

Avebury (StGB)

Stratford Saye (Va)

Lewisham (StPG)

Throwley (St BO)

Minster (StSA)

Stogursey (Lonlay)

Frampton (St EC)

Spettisbury (StPP)

Boxgrove (Ls)

Sele (St FS)

Folkestone (Lo)

Tywardreath (StSA)

Loders (Mn)

Runcton (Tr)

Tooting Bec (B-H)

Cowick (B-H)

Axmouth (Mn)

Wareham (Ly)

Arundel (Se)

Harmondsworth (StCdMR)

Totnes (StSA)

Wilmington (Gr)

Steventon (StMdPR)

Otterton (MStM)

Ellingham (StSlV)

Monks Sherborne (ClF)

Modbury (StPsD)

Clatford (StVeL)

Hayling (Ju)

St Michael's Mount (MStM)

Osbourne St George (BH)

Appuldurcombe (Mn)

Andover (StFdS)

Carisbrooke (Ly)

Upavon (StW)

C.Daniell

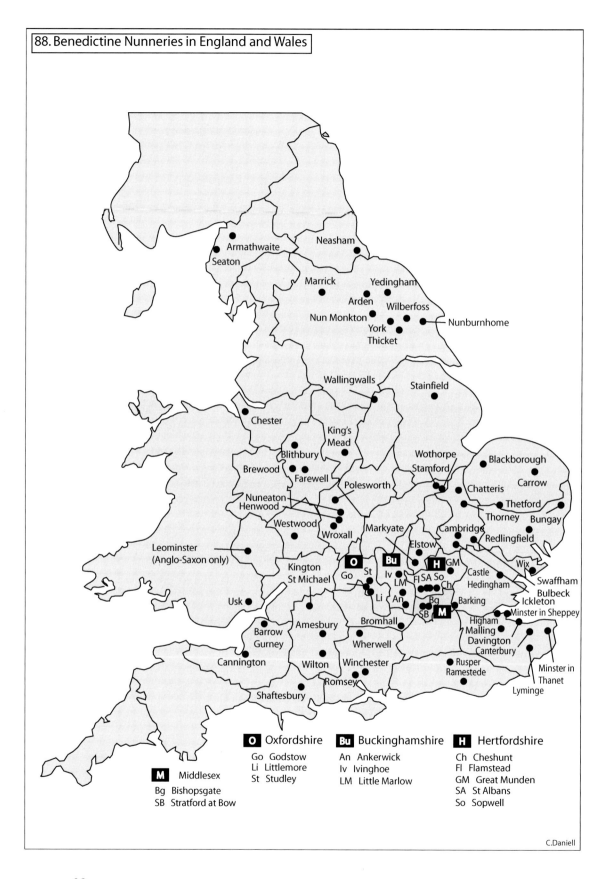

88. Benedictine Nunneries in England and Wales

Armathwaite
Seaton
Neasham
Marrick
Yedingham
Arden
Wilberfoss
Nun Monkton
York
Thicket
Nunburnhome
Wallingwalls
Stainfield
Chester
King's Mead
Blithbury
Wothorpe
Blackborough
Brewood
Farewell
Stamford
Carrow
Polesworth
Chatteris
Thetford
Nuneaton
Henwood
Thorney
Bungay
Westwood
Wroxall
Markyate
Cambridge
Redlingfield
Leominster
(Anglo-Saxon only)
Elstow
Wix
Kington
St Michael
O
Bu
H GM
Castle
Hedingham
Swaffham
Bulbeck
Go St
Iv
Usk
Li
An
FI SA So
Ch
Bg
Ickleton
Minster in Sheppey
LM
SB
M
Barking
Barrow
Gurney
Amesbury
Bromhall
Higham
Malling
Davington
Canterbury
Cannington
Wherwell
Wilton
Winchester
Rusper
Ramestede
Minster in
Thanet
Lyminge
Romsey
Shaftesbury

O Oxfordshire
Go Godstow
Li Littlemore
St Studley

Bu Buckinghamshire
An Ankerwick
Iv Ivinghoe
LM Little Marlow

H Hertfordshire
Ch Cheshunt
Fl Flamstead
GM Great Munden
SA St Albans
So Sopwell

M Middlesex
Bg Bishopsgate
SB Stratford at Bow

C.Daniell

98

89. Benedictine Monasteries in Scotland

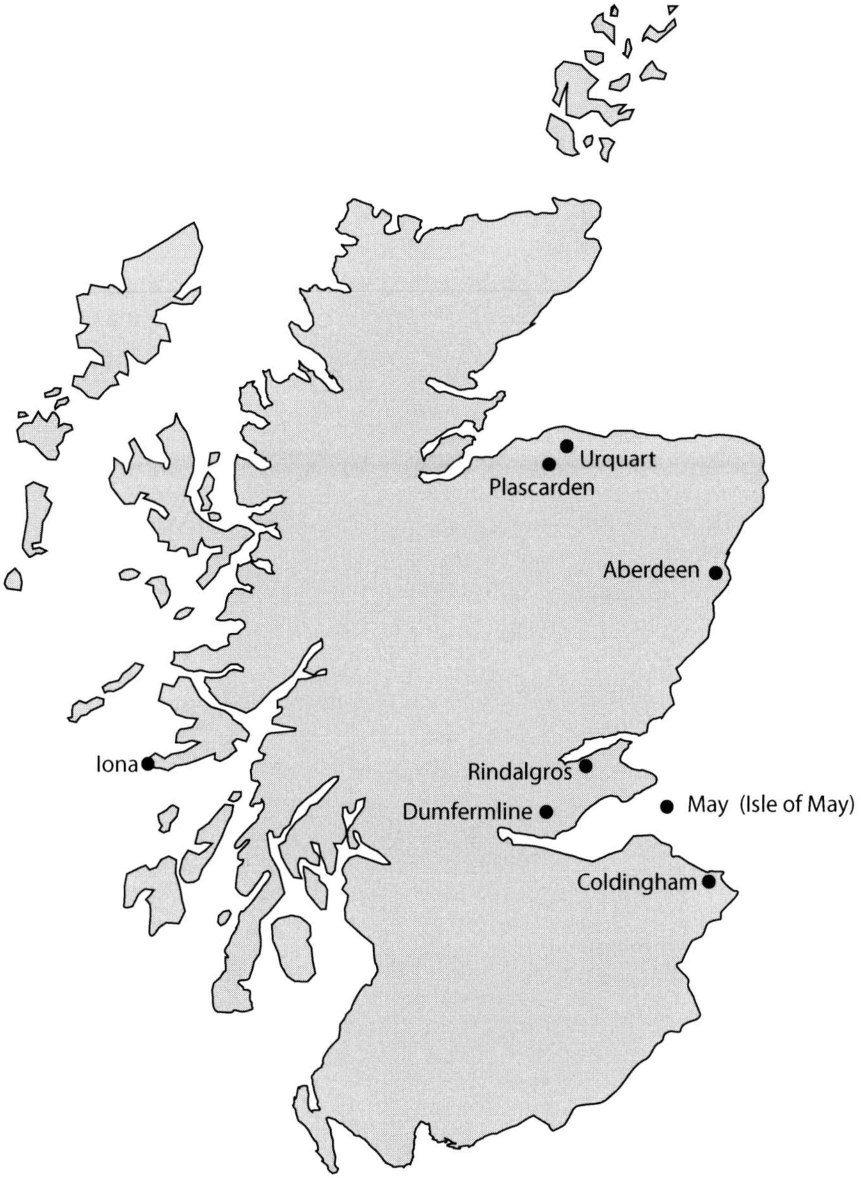

Urquart
Plascarden
Aberdeen
Iona
Rindalgros
May (Isle of May)
Dumfermline
Coldingham

C.Daniell

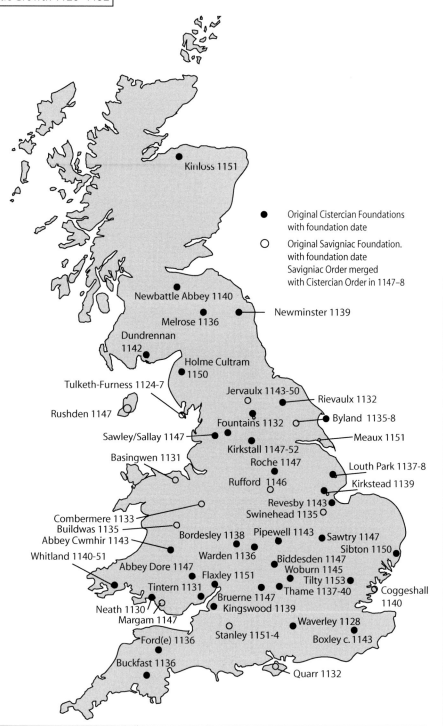

90. Cistercian Monastic Growth 1128–1152

● Original Cistercian Foundations with foundation date

○ Original Savigniac Foundation. with foundation date Savigniac Order merged with Cistercian Order in 1147–8

Kinloss 1151

Newbattle Abbey 1140
Melrose 1136
Newminster 1139
Dundrennan 1142
Holme Cultram 1150
Tulketh-Furness 1124-7
Jervaulx 1143-50
Rievaulx 1132
Rushden 1147
Byland 1135-8
Fountains 1132
Sawley/Sallay 1147
Meaux 1151
Kirkstall 1147-52
Basingwen 1131
Roche 1147
Louth Park 1137-8
Rufford 1146
Kirkstead 1139
Revesby 1143
Swinehead 1135
Combermere 1133
Buildwas 1135
Pipewell 1143
Abbey Cwmhir 1143
Bordesley 1138
Sawtry 1147
Whitland 1140-51
Warden 1136
Sibton 1150
Biddesden 1147
Abbey Dore 1147
Woburn 1145
Flaxley 1151
Tilty 1153
Tintern 1131
Thame 1137-40
Bruerne 1147
Coggeshall 1140
Neath 1130
Kingswood 1139
Margam 1147
Waverley 1128
Stanley 1151-4
Boxley c.1143
Ford(e) 1136
Buckfast 1136
Quarr 1132

The Cistercian Order is so called because it originated from Cîteaux in France and was founded in 1098. The Order interpreted the Rule of St Benedictine strictly and all houses were governed by the Cistercian General Chapter. The first English Cistercian abbey was at Rievaulx, founded in 1132. Thereafter the Order grew rapidly, and greatly increased in number with the affiliation of the Order of Savigny in 1147. In 1152 the General Chapter passed a decree banning further foundations, though this turned out not to be absolute.

C.Daniell

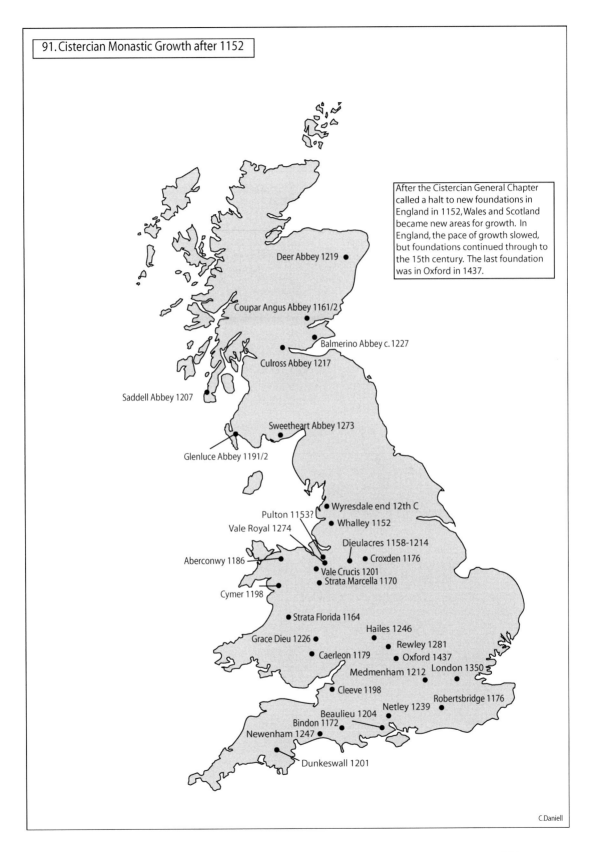

91. Cistercian Monastic Growth after 1152

After the Cistercian General Chapter called a halt to new foundations in England in 1152, Wales and Scotland became new areas for growth. In England, the pace of growth slowed, but foundations continued through to the 15th century. The last foundation was in Oxford in 1437.

Deer Abbey 1219

Coupar Angus Abbey 1161/2

Balmerino Abbey c. 1227

Culross Abbey 1217

Saddell Abbey 1207

Sweetheart Abbey 1273

Glenluce Abbey 1191/2

Wyresdale end 12th C

Pulton 1153?

Whalley 1152

Vale Royal 1274

Dieulacres 1158-1214

Croxden 1176

Aberconwy 1186

Vale Crucis 1201

Strata Marcella 1170

Cymer 1198

Strata Florida 1164

Hailes 1246

Grace Dieu 1226

Rewley 1281

Caerleon 1179

Oxford 1437

Medmenham 1212

London 1350

Cleeve 1198

Robertsbridge 1176

Netley 1239

Beaulieu 1204

Bindon 1172

Newenham 1247

Dunkeswall 1201

C.Daniell

101

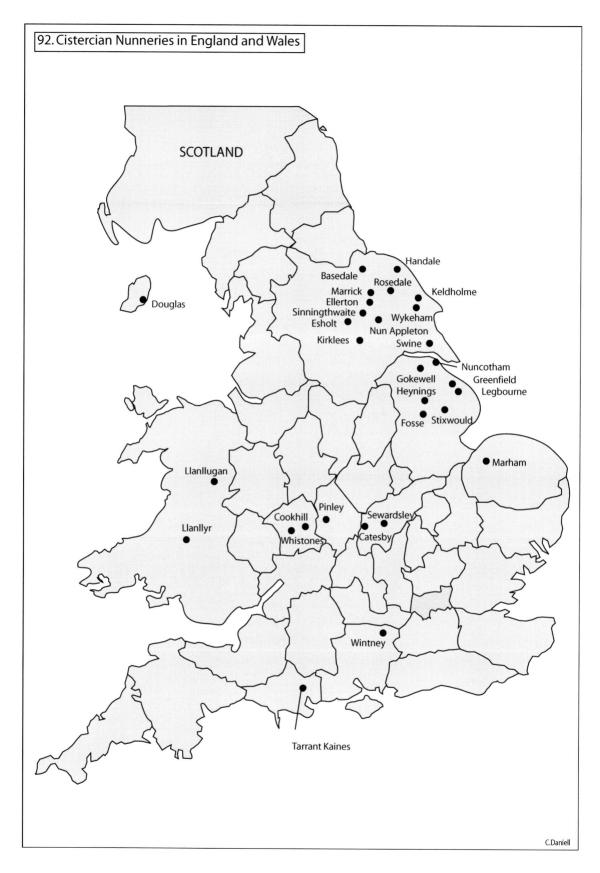

92. Cistercian Nunneries in England and Wales

SCOTLAND

Douglas

Handale
Basedale
Rosedale
Keldholme
Marrick
Ellerton
Sinningthwaite
Esholt
Wykeham
Nun Appleton
Kirklees
Swine
Nuncotham
Gokewell
Greenfield
Heynings
Legbourne
Fosse
Stixwould

Marham

Llanllugan

Pinley
Sewardsley
Cookhill
Catesby
Llanllyr
Whistones

Wintney

Tarrant Kaines

C.Daniell

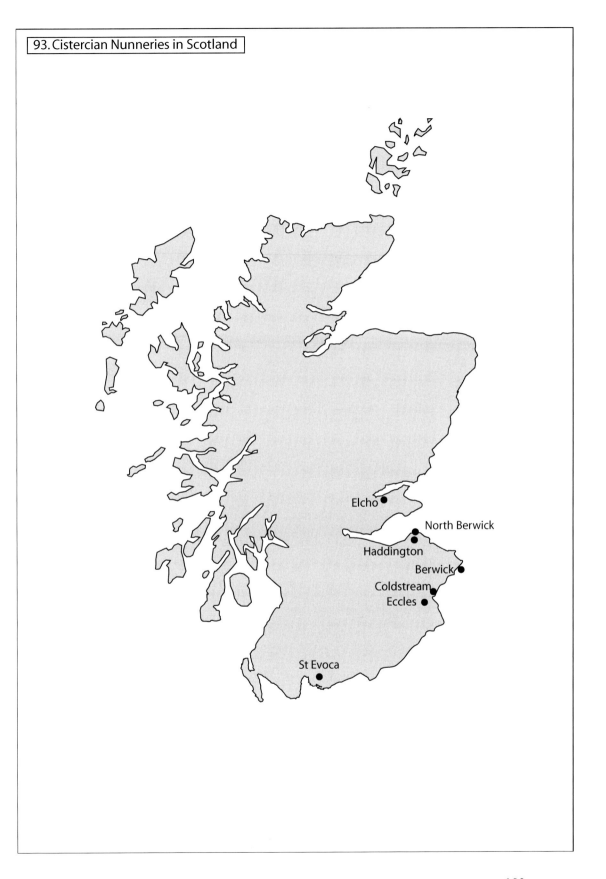

Elcho

North Berwick

Haddington

Berwick

Coldstream

Eccles

St Evoca

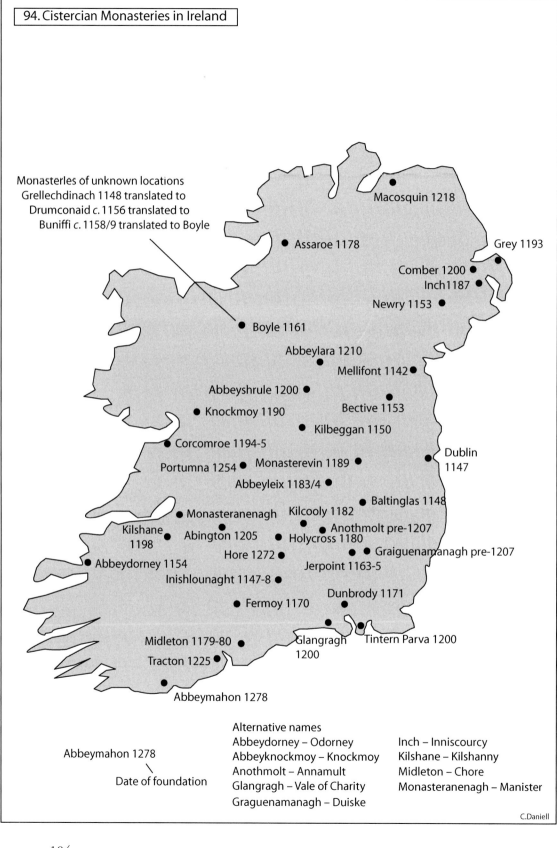

94. Cistercian Monasteries in Ireland

Macosquin 1218

Monasterles of unknown locations
Grellechdinach 1148 translated to
Drumconaid c.1156 translated to
Buniffi c.1158/9 translated to Boyle

Assaroe 1178

Grey 1193

Comber 1200
Inch1187

Newry 1153

Boyle 1161

Abbeylara 1210

Mellifont 1142

Abbeyshrule 1200

Bective 1153

Knockmoy 1190

Kilbeggan 1150

Corcomroe 1194-5

Dublin
1147

Portumna 1254

Monasterevin 1189

Abbeyleix 1183/4

Baltinglas 1148

Monasteranenagh

Kilcooly 1182

Kilshane
1198

Abington 1205

Anothmolt pre-1207

Holycross 1180

Hore 1272

Graiguenamanagh pre-1207

Abbeydorney 1154

Jerpoint 1163-5

Inishlounaght 1147-8

Dunbrody 1171

Fermoy 1170

Midleton 1179-80

Glangragh
1200

Tintern Parva 1200

Tracton 1225

Abbeymahon 1278

Abbeymahon 1278
\
Date of foundation

Alternative names
Abbeydorney – Odorney
Abbeyknockmoy – Knockmoy
Anothmolt – Annamult
Glangragh – Vale of Charity
Graguenamanagh – Duiske

Inch – Inniscourcy
Kilshane – Kilshanny
Midleton – Chore
Monasteranenagh – Manister

C.Daniell

95. Cluniac Monasteries and Nunneries in Great Britain

● Monastery
○ Nunneries

Paisley

Crossraguel

Arthington ○

Pontefract

Kersal

Monks Bretton

Normansburgh

Aldermanshaw

Bromholm

Derby

Lenton

Northampton

Castle Acre

Wenlock

Sleves Holm

Thetford

Preen

Dudley

Mendham

Daventry

Delapre

Wangford

Clifford

Preston
Capes

Newport
Pagnell

Little Horkesley

St Clears

Stanesgate

Prittlewell

Bermondsey

Monks Horton

Monkton
Farleigh

Barnstable

Montacute

Lewes

Kerswell

St Mawgan

Totnes

Holne

St Helens

St Carrok

The Cluniacs were named after their Burgundian motherhouse of Cluny, to which they were all bound. This in effect created a 'vast spiritual empire' across Europe, and it was a pattern also used by the more popular Cistercians. The first Cluniac monastery was at Lewes, founded in 1077. Though not numerous, the Cluniacs were the first wave of foundations after the Conquest.

C.Daniell

105

96. Carthusian Monasteries in Great Britain

Perth

Mount Grace

Hull

Axholme

Beauvale

Coventry

Hatherop

Lewisham

Hinton

Sheen

Witham

The Carthusians originated at Chartreuse (hence their name) high in the French Alps. They rejected the wealth being obtained by the other monastic orders and they emphasised isolation and spiritual striving. Witham was the first to be established in Britain, by Henry II as a penance for his murder of Thomas à Becket in 1170.

C.Daniell

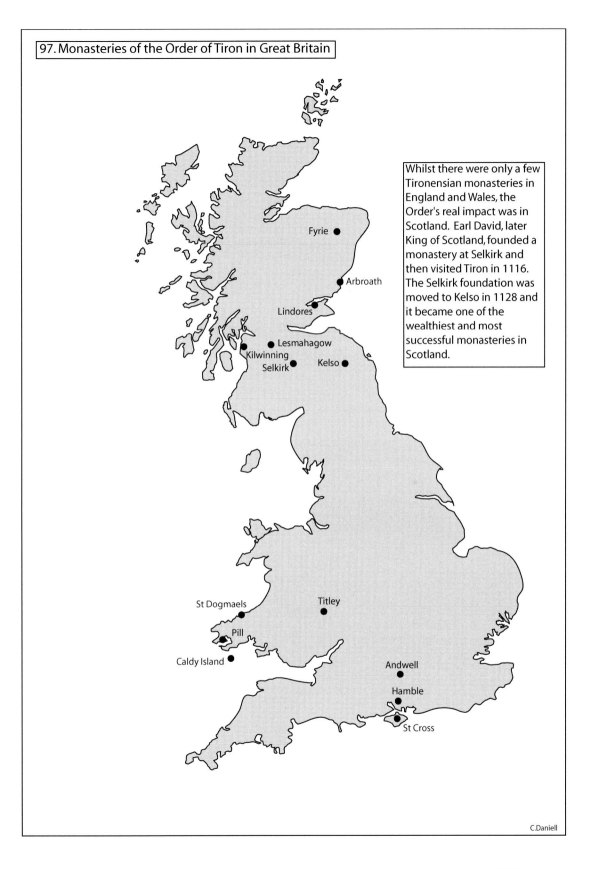

97. Monasteries of the Order of Tiron in Great Britain

Whilst there were only a few Tironensian monasteries in England and Wales, the Order's real impact was in Scotland. Earl David, later King of Scotland, founded a monastery at Selkirk and then visited Tiron in 1116. The Selkirk foundation was moved to Kelso in 1128 and it became one of the wealthiest and most successful monasteries in Scotland.

Fyrie

Arbroath

Lindores

Lesmahagow

Kilwinning

Selkirk

Kelso

St Dogmaels

Titley

Pill

Caldy Island

Andwell

Hamble

St Cross

C.Daniell

107

98. Austin (Augustinian) Monasteries in England and Wales

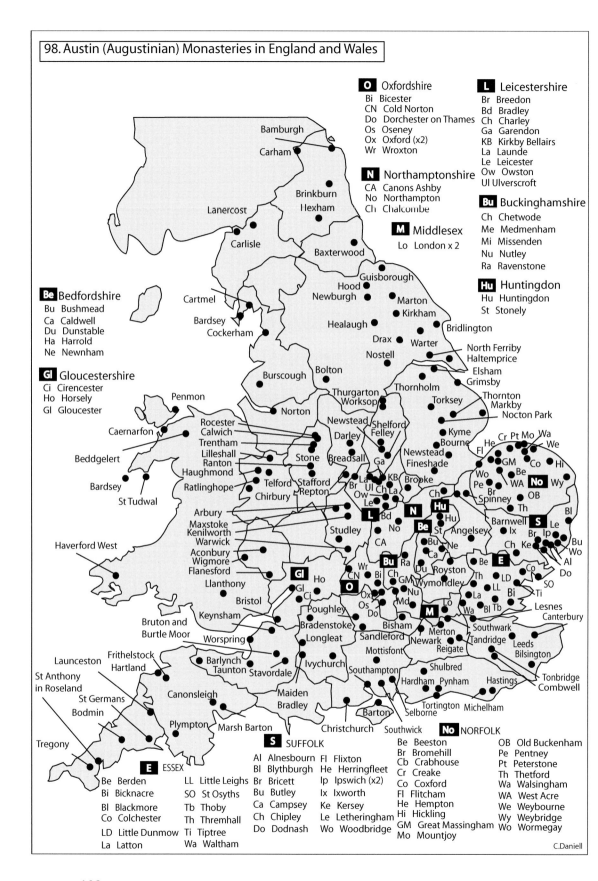

O Oxfordshire
Bi Bicester
CN Cold Norton
Do Dorchester on Thames
Os Oseney
Ox Oxford (x2)
Wr Wroxton

N Northamptonshire
CA Canons Ashby
No Northampton
Ch Chalcombe

M Middlesex
Lo London x 2

L Leicestershire
Br Breedon
Bd Bradley
Ch Charley
Ga Garendon
KB Kirkby Bellairs
La Launde
Le Leicester
Ow Owston
Ul Ulverscroft

Bu Buckinghamshire
Ch Chetwode
Me Medmenham
Mi Missenden
Nu Nutley
Ra Ravenstone

Hu Huntingdon
Hu Huntingdon
St Stonely

Be Bedfordshire
Bu Bushmead
Ca Caldwell
Du Dunstable
Ha Harrold
Ne Newnham

Gl Gloucestershire
Ci Cirencester
Ho Horsely
Gl Gloucester

No NORFOLK
Be Beeston
Br Bromehill
Cb Crabhouse
Cr Creake
Co Coxford
Fl Flitcham
He Hempton
Hi Hickling
GM Great Massingham
Mo Mountjoy
OB Old Buckenham
Pe Pentney
Pt Peterstone
Th Thetford
Wa Walsingham
WA West Acre
We Weybourne
Wy Weybridge
Wo Wormegay

S SUFFOLK
Al Alnesbourn
Bl Blythburgh
Br Bricett
Bu Butley
Ca Campsey
Ch Chipley
Do Dodnash
Fl Flixton
He Herringfleet
Ip Ipswich (x2)
Ix Ixworth
Ke Kersey
Le Letheringham
Wo Woodbridge

E ESSEX
Be Berden
Bi Bicknacre
Bl Blackmore
Co Colchester
LD Little Dunmow
La Latton
LL Little Leighs
SO St Osyths
Tb Thoby
Th Thremhall
Ti Tiptree
Wa Waltham

C.Daniell

99. Austin (Augustinian) Nunneries in England and Wales

Holystone

Moxby

Grimsby

Crabhouse

Brewood

Grace Dieu

Rothwell

Flixton

Aconbury

Harrold

Campsey

Burnham

London x 2

Goring

Bristol

Lacock

Minster in Sheppey

Easebourne

Canonsleigh

Cornworthy

The Austin, or Augustinian, communities of monks and nuns were so called because they followed the Rule attributed to St Augustine, Bishop of Hippo. The canons lived in common (as did the nuns), but played an active role in the community by preaching and caring for the sick. The greatest period of foundations was between 1100 and 1135. Henry I and his Queen, Matilda, were powerful advocates for them.

C.Daniell

Monymusk

Rethstenneth

Inchaffray
Strathfillian   Scone
Inchmahone   St Andrews
           Abernethy
Cambuskenneth   Pittenweem
         Loch Leven
Oronsay   Inchcolm
         Blantyre
                   Holyrood

                   Jedburgh

         Canonbie

St Mary's Isle

C.Danie

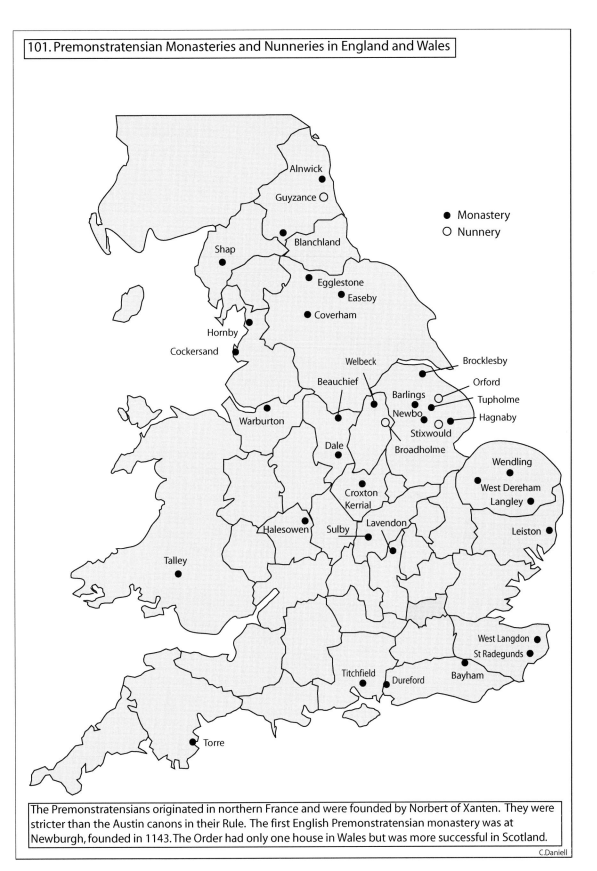

101. Premonstratensian Monasteries and Nunneries in England and Wales

- ● Monastery
- ○ Nunnery

Alnwick
Guyzance ○
Blanchland
Shap
Egglestone
Easeby
Coverham
Hornby
Cockersand
Welbeck
Beauchief
Brocklesby
Orford
Barlings
Tupholme
Newbo
Hagnaby
Warburton
Stixwould
Dale
Broadholme
Wendling
West Dereham
Langley
Croxton
Kerrial
Leiston
Halesowen
Sulby
Lavendon
Talley
West Langdon
St Radegunds
Titchfield
Dureford
Bayham
Torre

The Premonstratensians originated in northern France and were founded by Norbert of Xanten. They were stricter than the Austin canons in their Rule. The first English Premonstratensian monastery was at Newburgh, founded in 1143. The Order had only one house in Wales but was more successful in Scotland.

C.Daniell

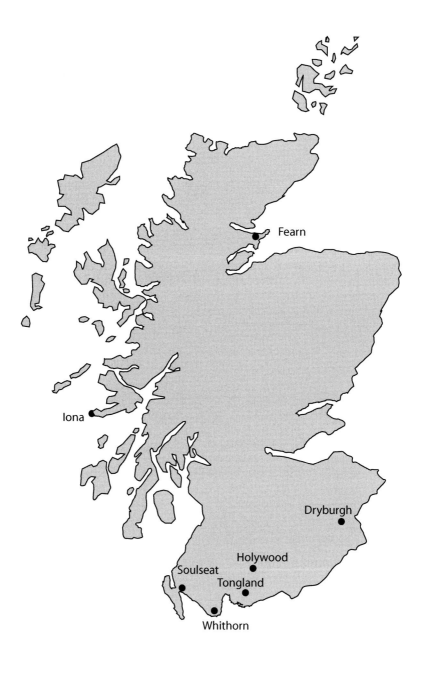

Fearn

Iona

Dryburgh

Holywood

Soulseat

Tongland

Whithorn

C.Daniell

103. Gilbertine Monasteries and Nunneries in Great Britain

- ● Gilbertine canons
- ○ Gilbertine double houses (canons and nuns)
- * Bullington originally canons only but joined by the nuns from Tunstall pre-1189

North Ormsby ○
Sixhills ○   ○ Alvingham
Bullington* ○
Lincoln ●

● Dalmilling

● Ravenstonedale

● Malton
York ●
○ Watton
Ellerton on Spalding Moor ●

Newstead ●

Mattersley ●

Haverholme
Holland Bridge

Catley ○

Sempringham

○ Shouldham
Marmont
Fordham

Clattercote
Chicksands
Cambridge

Poulton ●
Hitchin ●

Marlborough ●

The Gilbertine Order was founded by St Gilbert, who was the only Englishman to found a religious order. Gilbert encountered a number of women in his parish of Sempringham who wished to live an enclosed religious life. He therefore founded an enclosed convent, in which the sisters lived following the Benedictine Rule. Some men also wished to join, and these he placed under an Augustinian Rule. The Gilbertine Order was unusual, though not unique, in having joint double monasteries of canons and nuns on the same site, though they were strictly segregated. The Order was primarily based in Lincolnshire and Yorkshire with a scatter of monasteries elsewhere, but none overseas.

C.Daniell

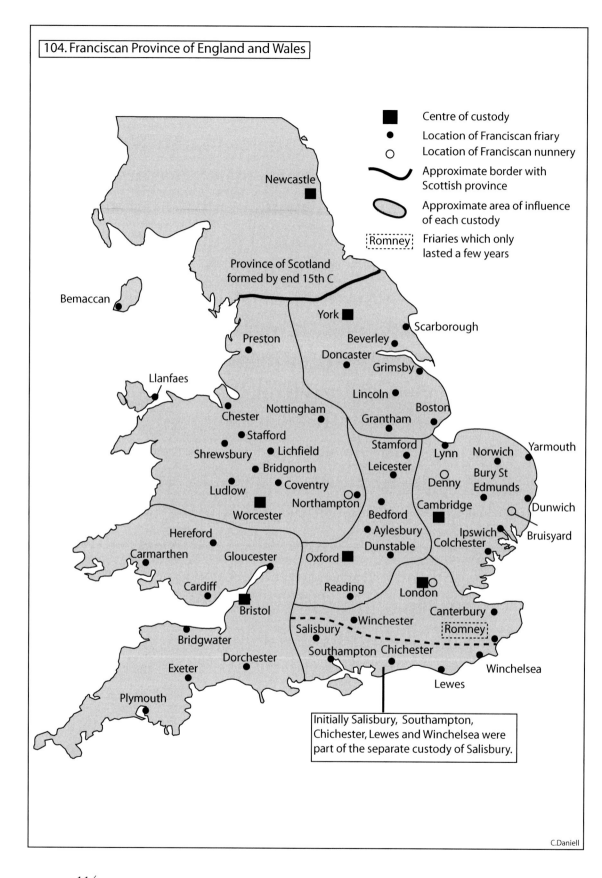

104. Franciscan Province of England and Wales

- ■ Centre of custody
- ● Location of Franciscan friary
- ○ Location of Franciscan nunnery
- Approximate border with Scottish province
- Approximate area of influence of each custody
- Romney — Friaries which only lasted a few years

Newcastle

Province of Scotland formed by end 15th C

Bemaccan

York
Scarborough
Preston
Beverley
Doncaster
Grimsby
Llanfaes
Lincoln
Boston
Nottingham
Chester
Grantham
Stafford
Stamford
Shrewsbury
Lichfield
Leicester
Lynn
Norwich
Yarmouth
Bridgnorth
Denny
Bury St Edmunds
Ludlow
Coventry
Northampton
Cambridge
Dunwich
Worcester
Bedford
Ipswich
Bruisyard
Hereford
Aylesbury
Colchester
Carmarthen
Gloucester
Dunstable
Cardiff
Oxford
Reading
London
Bristol
Canterbury
Bridgwater
Salisbury
Winchester
Romney
Dorchester
Southampton
Chichester
Winchelsea
Exeter
Lewes
Plymouth

Initially Salisbury, Southampton, Chichester, Lewes and Winchelsea were part of the separate custody of Salisbury.

C.Daniell

114

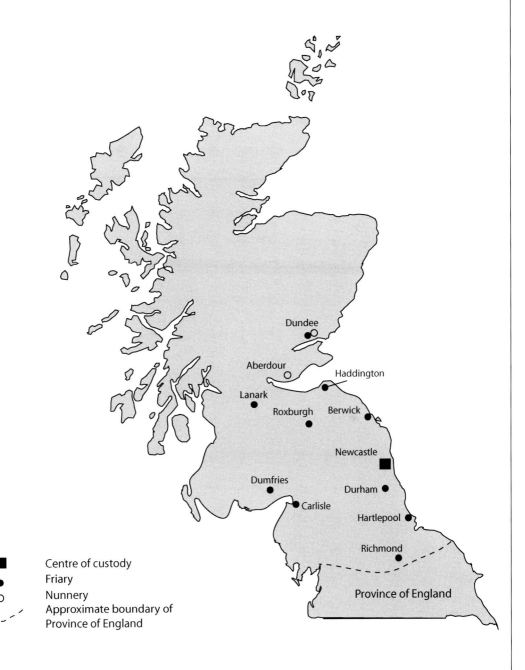

105. Franciscan Province of Scotland

Dundee

Aberdour

Haddington

Lanark

Roxburgh

Berwick

Newcastle

Dumfries

Durham

Carlisle

Hartlepool

Richmond

Province of England

■   Centre of custody
●   Friary
○   Nunnery
– – –   Approximate boundary of
Province of England

Predominantly created out of the custody of Newcastle, Scotland became briefly independent from England as an independent province c.1235. This was soon suppressed and Scotland became a vicariate between 1279 and 1296. Scotland became totally independent from the English province in 1329. By the end of the 15th century Scotland had gained the status of a province.

C. Daniell

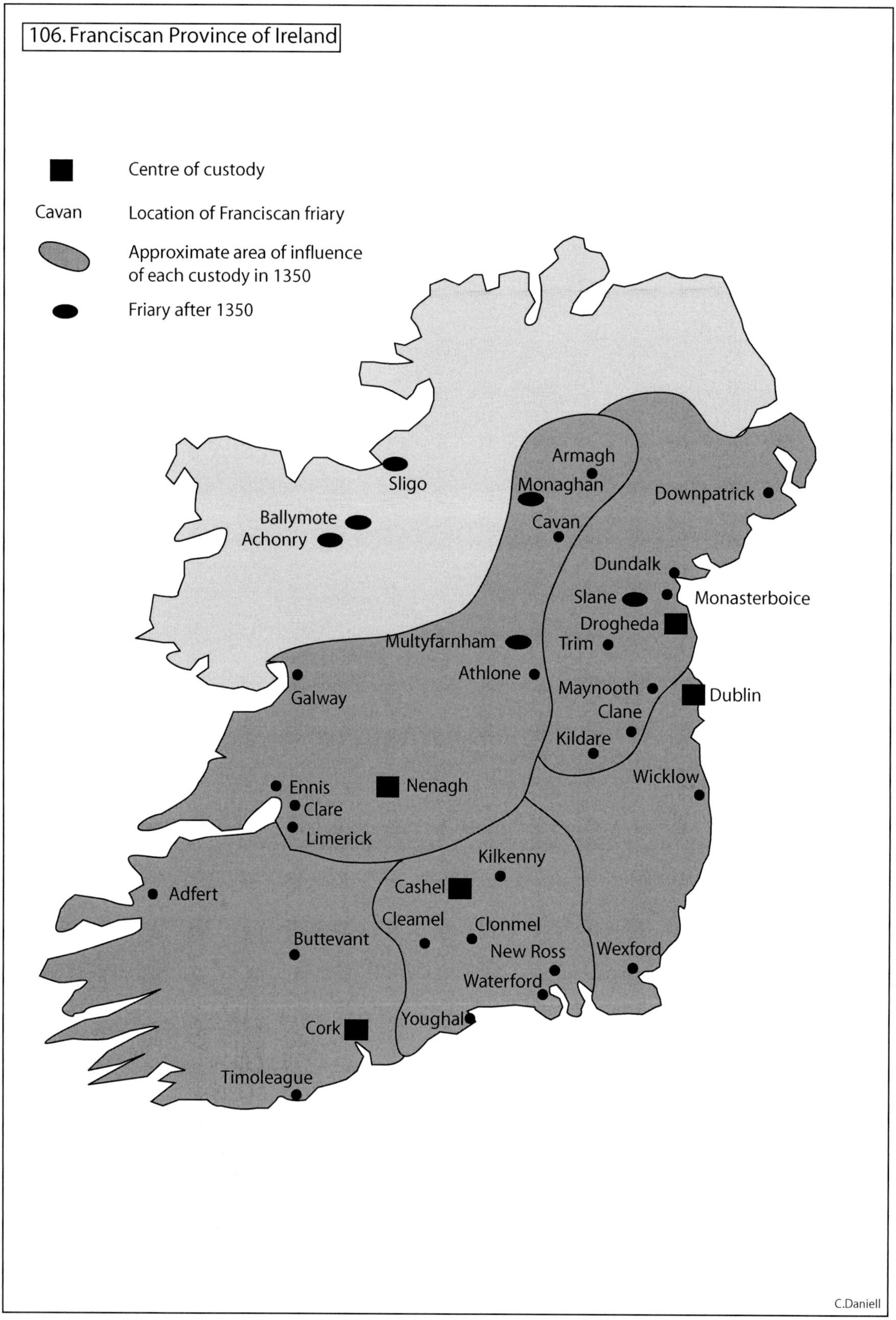

106. Franciscan Province of Ireland
Centre of custody
Cavan
Location of Franciscan friary
Approximate area of influence of each custody in 1350
Friary after 1350
Sligo
Ballymote
Achonry
Armagh
Monaghan
Downpatrick
Cavan
Dundalk
Slane
Monasterboice
Drogheda
Multyfarnham
Trim
Athlone
Galway
Maynooth
Dublin
Clane
Kildare
Wicklow
Ennis
Nenagh
Clare
Limerick
Kilkenny
Cashel
Adfert
Cleamel
Clonmel
Buttevant
New Ross
Wexford
Waterford
Youghal
Cork
Timoleague
C.Daniell

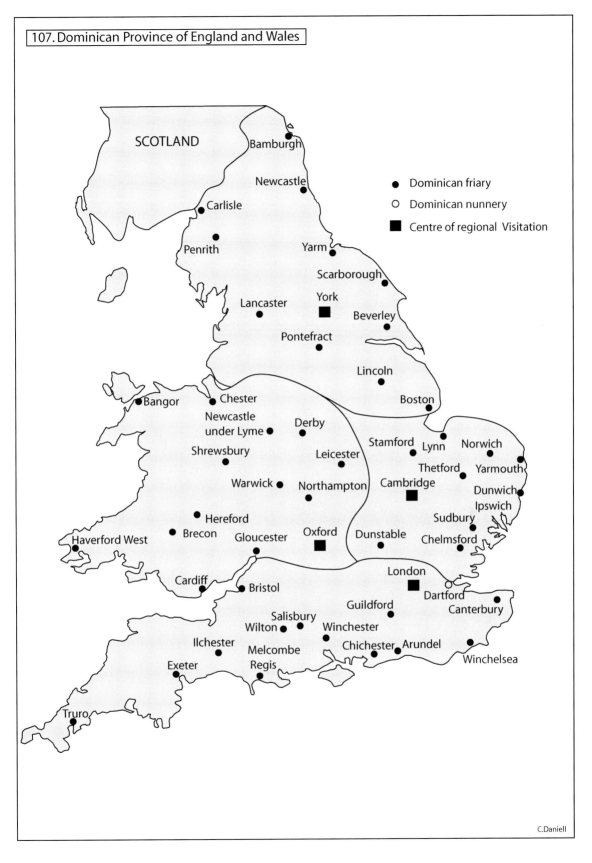

107. Dominican Province of England and Wales

SCOTLAND

Bamburgh

Newcastle

Carlisle

Penrith

Yarm

Scarborough

York

Beverley

Lancaster

Pontefract

Lincoln

● Dominican friary
○ Dominican nunnery
■ Centre of regional Visitation

Bangor

Chester

Boston

Newcastle under Lyme

Derby

Stamford

Lynn

Norwich

Shrewsbury

Leicester

Thetford

Yarmouth

Warwick

Northampton

Cambridge

Dunwich

Ipswich

Hereford

Sudbury

Brecon

Oxford

Dunstable

Chelmsford

Haverford West

Gloucester

Cardiff

Bristol

London

Dartford

Guildford

Canterbury

Salisbury

Winchester

Wilton

Ilchester

Chichester

Arundel

Melcombe Regis

Winchelsea

Exeter

Truro

C.Daniell

117

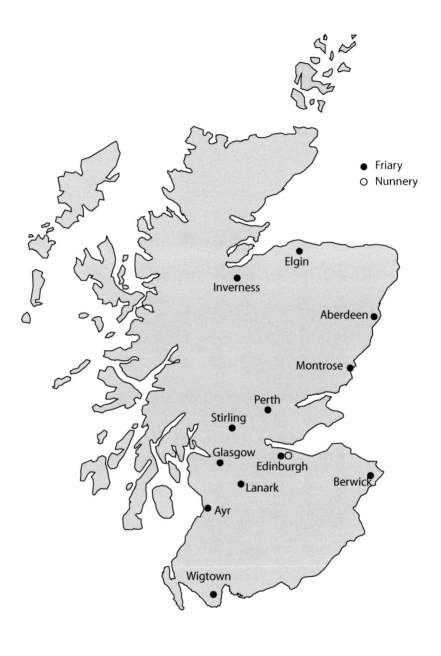

108. Dominican Province of Scotland

● Friary
○ Nunnery

Elgin
Inverness
Aberdeen
Montrose
Perth
Stirling
Glasgow
Edinburgh
Berwick
Lanark
Ayr
Wigtown

C.Daniell

118

Strade

Derry

Coleraine

Newtownards

Rathran

Sligo

Ballindown

Burrishoole

Clocnamechan

Clonshanville

Urlaur

Dundalk

Carlingford

Longford

Roscommon

Mullingar

Trim

Toombeola

Galway

Athenry

Portumna

Lorna

Athy

Aghaboe

Arklow

Kilkenny

Kilmallock

Tralee

New Ross

Carelyons

Youghal

C.Daniell

119

Berwick is the northernmost friary; there are no Austin friaries in Scotland

SCOTLAND

Berwick

Newcastle

Penrith

Barnard Castle

Northallerton

York

Tickhill

Hull

Grimsby

Warrington

Lincoln

Boston

Woodhouse

Shrewsbury

Stafford

Atherstone

Stamford

Lynn

Norwich

Yarmouth
Gorleston

Droitwich

Huntingdon

Thetford

Cambridge

Ludlow

Northampton

Clare

Orford

Newport

Oxford

London

Bristol

Canterbury

Sherborne

Winchester

Rye

C.Daniell

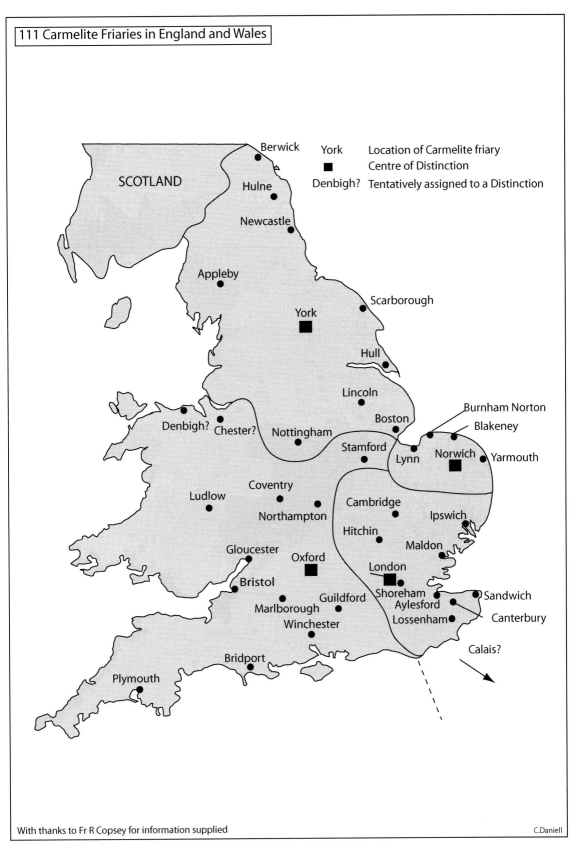

111 Carmelite Friaries in England and Wales

York — Location of Carmelite friary
■ — Centre of Distinction
Denbigh? — Tentatively assigned to a Distinction

SCOTLAND

Berwick
Hulne
Newcastle
Appleby
Scarborough
York
Hull
Lincoln
Boston
Burnham Norton
Blakeney
Denbigh?
Chester?
Nottingham
Stamford
Lynn
Norwich
Yarmouth
Coventry
Cambridge
Ludlow
Ipswich
Northampton
Hitchin
Gloucester
Maldon
Oxford
London
Bristol
Shoreham
Guildford
Aylesford
Sandwich
Marlborough
Lossenham
Canterbury
Winchester
Calais?
Bridport
Plymouth

With thanks to Fr R Copsey for information supplied

C.Daniell

121

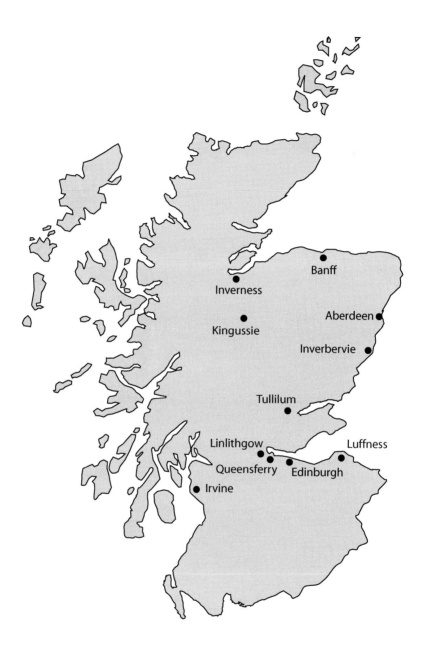

Banff

Inverness

Kingussie

Aberdeen

Inverbervie

Tullilum

Linlithgow

Luffness

Queensferry

Edinburgh

Irvine

Scotland was theoretically made an independent Carmelite province from England in 1303, but took until 1311 to become a vicariate, and in 1324 became a formal province and retained this status thereafter.

C.Daniell

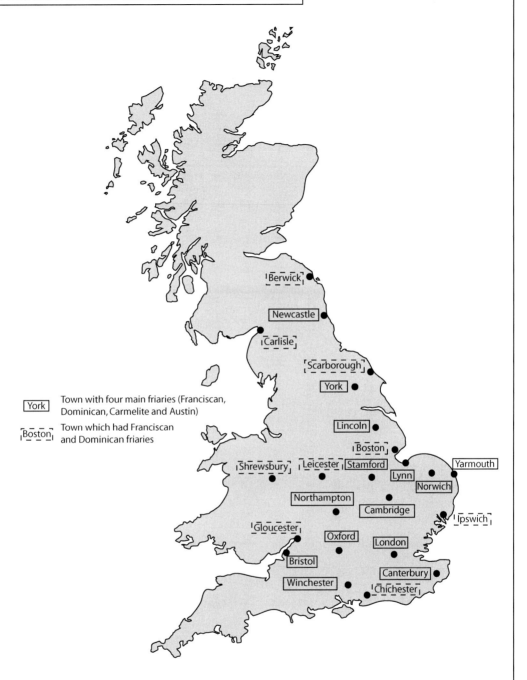

113. Towns with Four Main Orders of Friars in Great Britain

York — Town with four main friaries (Franciscan, Dominican, Carmelite and Austin)

Boston — Town which had Franciscan and Dominican friaries

Berwick
Newcastle
Carlisle
Scarborough
York
Lincoln
Boston
Yarmouth
Shrewsbury   Leicester   Stamford
Lynn
Norwich
Northampton
Cambridge
Ipswich
Gloucester
Oxford
London
Bristol
Winchester
Canterbury
Chichester

Friars originated in Italy and France in the early 13th century and quickly spread throughout Europe. They rejected the solitude and increasing wealth of the monastic orders and were primarily based in larger towns. Their collective name was 'mendicant friars' (*mendicans* – begging) as originally they survived by begging, but by the later Middle Ages the friars had acquired some property and wealth. The Franciscans were named after St Francis, Dominicans after St Dominic, Carmelites after Mount Carmel where they were founded, and Austin (or Augustinian) Friars were so called because they followed the Rule of St Augustine.

C.Daniell

114. Minor Orders of Friars in Great Britain

Legend:
- ● Friars of the Sack
- ○ Crutched Friars
- ⊕ Pied Friars
- ⊖ Friars de Ordine Martyrum

Locations:
Berwick
Newcastle
Kildale
York
Lincoln
Chester
Whaplode
Stamford
Leicester
Lynn
Barham
Norwich
Worcester
Northampton
Cambridge
Welnetham
Oxford
Colchester
Wotton under Edge
Bristol
London
Ospringe
Donnington
Guildford
Reigate
Canterbury
Rye

C.Daniell

Torphichen

Castleboy

Mount St John

Kilmainham Wood
Kilmainhambeg
Kilsaran

Newland   Beverley

Kilmainham
Killybegs
Tully
Kilteel

Ossington   Maltby

Ysbyty-Ifan   Yeaveley   Skirbeck
Halston   Dalby

Dingley
Carbrooke

Clonoulty
Hospital
Mourne   Ballyhack
Crooke

Dinmore   Chippenham

Melchbourne   Battisford

Cork

Shingay
Querington   Grafton   Standon
Hogshaw

Slebech   Cranfield   Clerkenwell

Sutton

Godsfield   Swingfield
Boddiscombe   Ansty   Poling
Buckland   Fryer Mayne

Trebeigh

The Knights Hospitaller were founded after the First Crusade in 1095 to care for those in the hospital at Jerusalem. The Order gained Papal approval in 1113 and soon expanded its role to providing armed protection for pilgrims. Like the Templars, the Hospitallers became an effective fighting force. A European-wide organisation was founded to fund their operations. The Hospitallers gained the property of the Templars after the latter's fall in 1312. The Hospitallers were forced out of the Holy Land by the victorious Muslims and firstly settled on Cyprus, then Rhodes and finally, in the 16th century, Malta. In the British Isles their lands were seized in the Reformation.

C.Daniell

116. Knights Templar Preceptories and Hospitals

- Preceptory
- H Hospital

Maryculter

Balantrodoch

Thornton

Westerdale
Cowton
Penhill
Foulbridge
Copmanthorpe
Ribston
Wetherby
Temple Newsam
Faxfleet
Temple Hirst

Temple House
Templetown
Clontarf
Dublin
Kildare
Kilkenny
Waterford
Wexford

Willoughton
Eagle H Mere
Temple Bruer
Keele South Witham
Rothley
Aslackby
Temple Balsall
Great
Lydley Denny Abbey Wilbraham
H
Temple Duxford
Upleden Guiting Dunwich
Garway Cowley Temple Dinsley
Sandford Cressing Temple
London
Redcliffe Temple
Temple Rockley Ewell
Temple Combe Seddlescombe Shipley

The Knights Templar were founded after the First Crusade in 1095 in order to protect pilgrims arriving in the Holy Land, and later they became a large and effective fighting force. The Order was confirmed by the Pope in 1128. To fund its operations and gain recruits the Order launched a widescale recruiting drive, rapidly gaining membership, wealth and power. However, the Templars were often unpopular and in 1307 Philip IV of France had members of the Order arrested. Other monarchies quickly followed and in 1312 the Order was suppressed by the Papacy and their lands were transferred to the Knights Hospitallers.

C.Daniell

117. Larger Jewish Communities in England

- ● Medieval Jewish cemeteries indicating larger communities of Jews
- 🔥 Attacks on Jews or Jewish communities 1190

York

Lincoln

King's Lynn

Stamford

Norwich

Northampton

Cambridge

Oxford

London

Bristol

Canterbury

Winchester

During the Anglo-Saxon era individual Jews may have visited England, but it was only after the Norman Conquest that William the Conqueror actively encouraged Jewish communities to settle. Jewish communities were based in the towns and the larger communities were allowed cemeteries. In York the Jewish cemetery of Jewbury has been archaeologically excavated. The Jews were the king's property and they could be taxed as much as the king liked. For centuries they were an important source of taxation revenue, especially as through business and money-lending individual Jews became incredibly wealthy. In 1190 anti-Jewish sentiment was so intense that attacks and massacres of Jews took place, the worst occurring in York. By the end of the 14th century the kings had taxed the Jewish communities into a state of poverty. In 1290 Edward I expelled all the Jews from England and Jewish communities did not return until 1653.

C.Daniell

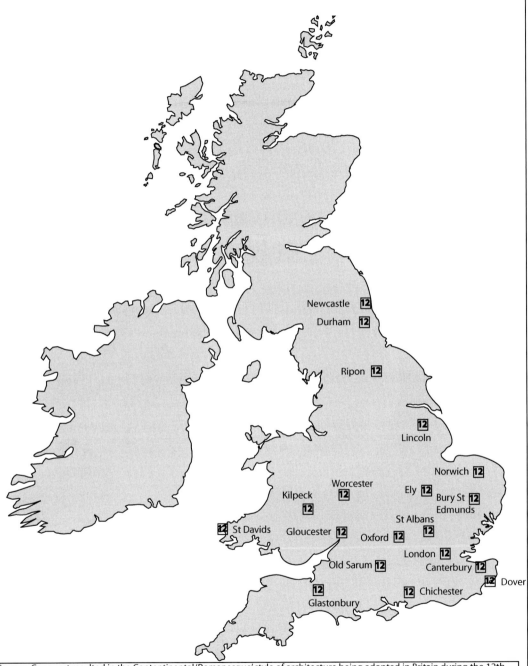

118. Major Architectural Sites of the 12th Century

Newcastle **12**

Durham **12**

Ripon **12**

12
Lincoln

Norwich **12**

Worcester
12

Kilpeck
12

Ely **12**

Bury St **12**
Edmunds

12 St Davids

Gloucester **12**

St Albans
12

Oxford **12**

London **12**

Old Sarum **12**

Canterbury **12**

12 Dover

12
Glastonbury

12 Chichester

The Norman Conquest resulted in the Contentinental 'Romanesque' style of architecture being adopted in Britain during the 12th century, so called in the 19th century because it was seen to follow Roman style. The Normans instigated a massive building programme of churches and castles. Examples of Romanesque architecture include the White Tower (1078) – the original keep of the Tower of London – and St Albans Abbey (now Cathedral), Norwich Cathedral and sections of Chichester, Gloucester and Ely Cathedrals. Durham Cathedral (1093–c. 1130) is built in the Romanesque style, but with innovations leading to the Gothic style of the following centuries. By the end of the century the Gothic 'Early English' style of architecture was becoming more fashionable.

C.Daniell

Kirkwall

13 Elgin

Dunblane
13

13 Glasgow
13 Holyrood

Durham 13

York 13

Dublin
Kildare 13   13

13
Lincoln

Southwell 13

13 Kilkenny

13 Lichfield

Cashel 13

13 Worcester

Llanthony 13

Waltham
13

Windsor
13   13
London

Salisbury
13 Canterbury

13   13
Wells

The predominant style of architecture at the beginning of the 13th century was the Gothic 'Early English' style, but by mid-century this had evolved into the Gothic 'Decorated' style. (The names of styles are later creations – it is not known what the Medieval architects called their styles.) One trait of the Early English style are the simple, elongated lancet windows. The style began with the east end of Canterbury Cathedral, built in the mid-1170s, and reached a peak in the cathedrals of Salisbury, Wells and Lincoln.

C.Daniell

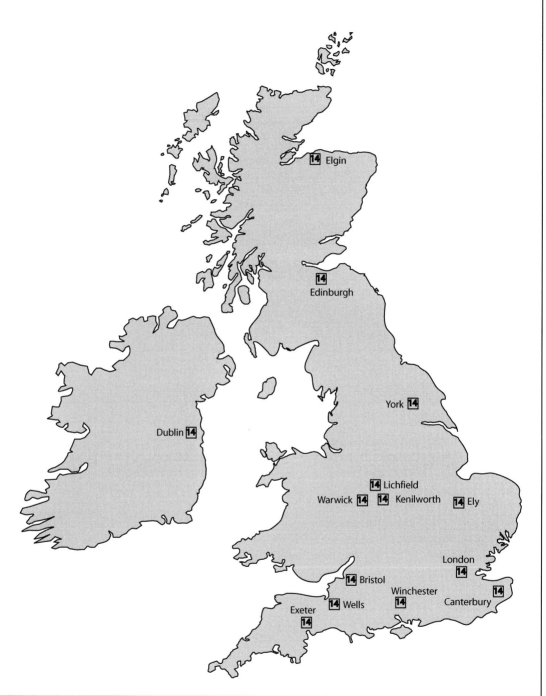

120. Major Architectural Sites of the 14th Century

14 Elgin

14 Edinburgh

York **14**

Dublin **14**

14 Lichfield

Warwick **14** | **14** Kenilworth

14 Ely

London **14**

14 Bristol

Winchester **14**

14 Canterbury

14 Wells

Exeter **14**

Gothic 'Decorated' architecture (late-13th–14th century), introduced a greater richness and complexity of carving, in particular in the intricate tracery of church windows. Exeter Cathedral is a suberb example of a church built in the Decorated style. In the mid-14th century the Black Death devastated the country, but it is often difficult to see its effect on the building programmes from the fabric alone.

C.Daniell

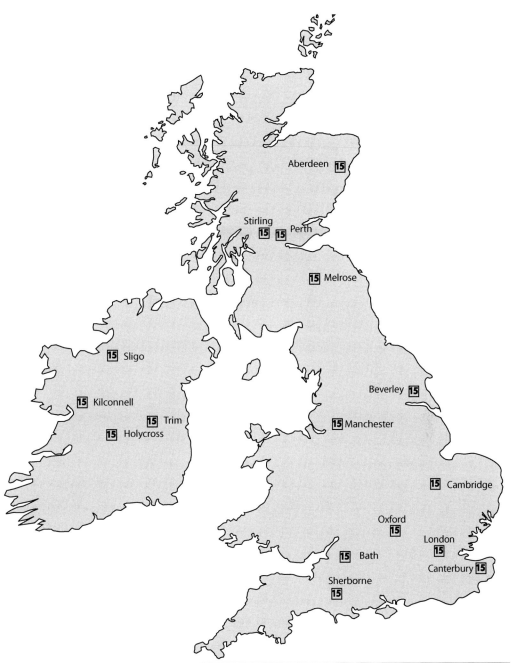

Aberdeen 15

Stirling 15 15 Perth

15 Melrose

15 Sligo

Beverley 15

15 Kilconnell

15 Trim

15 Manchester

15 Holycross

15 Cambridge

Oxford
15

London
15

15 Bath

Canterbury 15

Sherborne
15

Gothic 'Perpendicular' architecture (14th–mid-16th century) is a style which stresses the vertical lines of a building. The style is easily seen in the tracery of church windows where the mullions run in lines from top to bottom. The Perpendicular style therefore shows a unity of style, very different to the creative curves of the Decorated period. By the end of the century a new style was evolving, shown by spectacular 'fan vaulting' at Bath and Cambridge. Church building effectively stopped following the Reformation and the dismantling of the church by Henry VIII in the mid-16th century.

C. Daniell

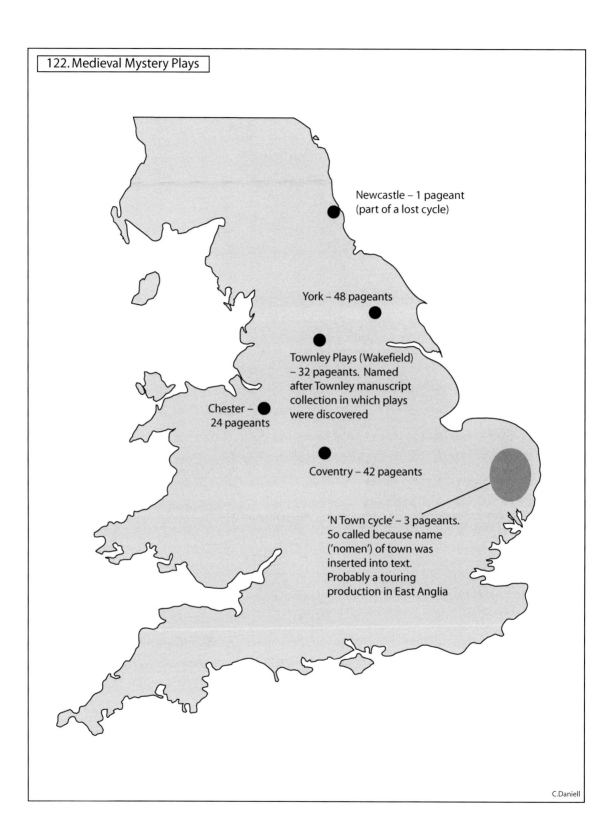

Newcastle – 1 pageant
(part of a lost cycle)

York – 48 pageants

Townley Plays (Wakefield)
– 32 pageants. Named
after Townley manuscript
collection in which plays
were discovered

Chester –
24 pageants

Coventry – 42 pageants

'N Town cycle' – 3 pageants.
So called because name
('nomen') of town was
inserted into text.
Probably a touring
production in East Anglia

C.Daniell

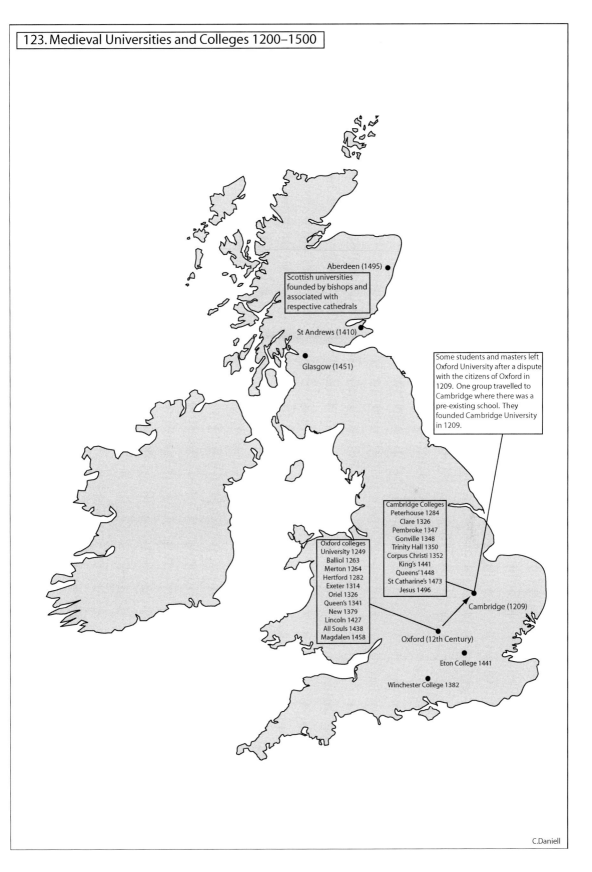

Aberdeen (1495) ●

Scottish universities
founded by bishops and
associated with
respective cathedrals

St Andrews (1410) ●

Glasgow (1451) ●

Some students and masters left
Oxford University after a dispute
with the citizens of Oxford in
1209. One group travelled to
Cambridge where there was a
pre-existing school. They
founded Cambridge University
in 1209.

Cambridge Colleges
Peterhouse 1284
Clare 1326
Pembroke 1347
Gonville 1348
Trinity Hall 1350
Corpus Christi 1352
King's 1441
Queens' 1448
St Catharine's 1473
Jesus 1496

Oxford colleges
University 1249
Balliol 1263
Merton 1264
Hertford 1282
Exeter 1314
Oriel 1326
Queen's 1341
New 1379
Lincoln 1427
All Souls 1438
Magdalen 1458

Cambridge (1209)

Oxford (12th Century)

Eton College 1441

Winchester College 1382

C.Daniell

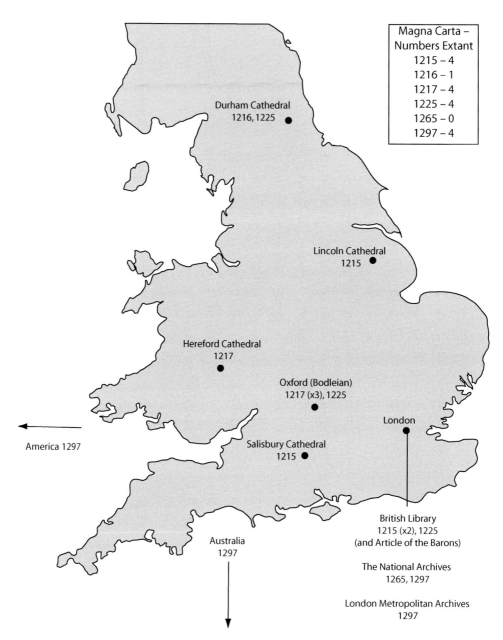

124. Current Locations of Magna Carta

Magna Carta –
Numbers Extant
1215 – 4
1216 – 1
1217 – 4
1225 – 4
1265 – 0
1297 – 4

Durham Cathedral
1216, 1225

Lincoln Cathedral
1215

Hereford Cathedral
1217

Oxford (Bodleian)
1217 (x3), 1225

London

America 1297

Salisbury Cathedral
1215

Australia
1297

British Library
1215 (x2), 1225
(and Article of the Barons)

The National Archives
1265, 1297

London Metropolitan Archives
1297

Magna Carta was first assented to by King John in 1215. The original is now lost, but an early draft, the Article of the Barons, still exists. Contemporary copies of Magna Carta were sent to the Royal Archives, the Cinque Ports and 40 counties. Only four of 1215 now survive, each slightly different. In times of crisis it was re-issued (with amendments), and it became standard for a king to assent to it on his coronation, a tradition which continued until Henry V. The relevance of Magna Carta then faded (Shakespeare does not mention it in his play *King John*) but Magna Carta became a critical document in the 17th century when Parliament was in dispute with King Charles I.

C. Daniell

BIBLIOGRAPHY

C.T. Allmand, *The Hundred Years War*, Cambridge, 1988.

M. Barber, *The New Knighthood, A History of the Order of the Temple*, Cambridge, 1998

M. Barber, *The Trial of the Templars*, Cambridge, 2006.

C.M. Barron, *London in the Later Middle Ages: Government and People 1200–1500*, Oxford, 2005.

R. Bartlett, *England under the Norman and Angevin Kings, 1075–1225*, Oxford, 2000.

M. Beresford, *The Lost Villages of England*, Stroud, 1998.

M. Beresford and H.P.R. Finberg, *Early Medieval Borough Handlist*, Newton Abbot, 1973.

J. Burton, *The Monastic and Religious Orders in Britain, 1000–1300*, Cambridge, 1994.

B.M.S. Campbell, J.A. Galloway, D. Keene and Margaret Murphy, *A Medieval Capital and its Grain Supply: Agrarian Production and its Distribution in the London Region, c. 1300*, Historical Geography Research Series, 1993.

J. Campbell, E. John and P. Wormald, *The Anglo-Saxons*, Harmondsworth, 1991.

D. Ó Cróinín, *Early Medieval Ireland, AD 400–1200*, London, 1995.

B. Cunliffe, *The Ancient Celts*, Harmondsworth, 1999.

C. Daniell, *From Norman Conquest to Magna Carta*, Abingdon, 2003.

R.R. Davis, *The Age of Conquest, Wales 1063–1415*, Oxford, 1991.

D. Ditchburn, S. Maclean and A. Mackay (eds), *Atlas of Medieval Europe*, Abingdon, 2007.

R. Dobson (ed.), *The Peasants' Revolt of 1381*, London, 1983.

S. Duffy, *Ireland in the Middle Ages*, Basingstoke, 1996.

D.E. Esson, *The Medieval Religious Houses of Scotland*, London, 1957.

R. Frame, *The Political Development of the British Isles 1100–1400*, Oxford, 1990.

S. Frere, *Britannia: History of Roman Britain*, London, 1991.

J. Gillingham, *The Wars of the Roses*, London, 2001.

J. Graham-Campbell and D. Kydd, *The Vikings*, London 1980.

N. Higham, *The Death of Anglo-Saxon England*, Stroud, 1997.

D. Hill, *An Atlas of Anglo-Saxon England*, Oxford, Repr. 1989.

P. Hindle, *Medieval Roads and Tracks*, Princes Risborough, 1998.

R. Horrox, *The Black Death*, Manchester, 2004.

M. Kowaleski, *Local Markets and Regional Trade in Medieval Exeter*, Cambridge, 1995.

D. Knowles, *The Monastic Order in England*, Oxford, 1966.

D. Knowles, *Medieval Religious Houses in England and Wales*, Oxford, 1971.

C. Lawrence, *The Friars*, London 1994.

C. H. Lawrence, *Medieval Monasticism*, Harlow, 2001.

J.M. Lilley et al. *The Jewish Burial Ground at Jewbury, York*, York, 1994.

P. McNeill and R. Nicholson, *An Historical Atlas of Scotland c. 400– c. 1600*, St Andrews, 1975.

T.E. McNeil, *Castles*, London, 1992.

A. Martindale, *Gothic Art*, London 1986.

E. Miller and J. Hatcher, *Medieval England, Towne, Commerce and Crafts 1086–1348*, London, 1995.

T. O'Keefe, *Medieval Ireland: An Archaeology*, Stroud, 2001.

D.M. Palliser (ed.) *The Cambridge Urban History of Britain, Vol. I, 600–1540*, Cambridge, 2000.

P. Skinner, *Jews in Medieval Britain: Historical, Literary and Archaeological Perspectives*, Woodbridge, 2003.

J. Sumption, *The Hundred Years War: Trial by Battle*, London, 1990.

J. Sumption, *The Hundred Years War: Trial by Fire*, London, 1999.

P. Ziegler, *The Black Death*, Stroud, 2003.

INDEX

Argyll and Tarbert, sheriffdom 4
Arklow, Dominican friary 109
Armagh 7, diocese of 85, Franciscan friary 106
Armathwaite, Benedictine nunnery 88
Arthington, Cluniac nunnery 95
Article of the Barons 124
Arundel, alien Benedictine monastery 87, Dominican friary 107, Earl of 29
Aslackby, Templar house 116
Assaroe, Cistercian nunnery 94
Astley, alien Benedictine monastery 87
Athelney, Benedictine monastery 86
Athelstan, King 13
Athenry, battle of 33, castle 48, Dominican friary 109
Atherstone 55, Austin friary 110
Athlone, Franciscan friary 106
Athy, Dominican friary 109
Atiscross 17
Atrebates 8
Augustinian Friars - see Austin Friars
Auld Alliance 44
Aumale 87
Austin Friars 110, 113
Australia 124
Avebury, alien Benedictine monastery 87
Axbridge 12
Axholme, Carthusian monastery 96
Axmouth, alien Benedictine monastery 87
Aylesbury, Franciscan friary 104
Aylesford, Carmelite friary 111
Ayr 5, 32, Dominican friary 108, mint 63, sheriffdom 4

Balliol College, Oxford, parliament 45
Balliol, John, King of Scotland 31, 34
Balantrodoch, Templar house 116
Ball, John 38
Ballindown, Dominican friary 109
Ballyhack, Hospitaller house 115
Ballymote, castle 48, Franciscan friary 106
Balmerino, Cistercian monastery 91
Baltinglas, Cistercian nunnery 94
Bamburgh, Austin monastery 98, castle 48, Dominican friary 107, mint 61
Banff 31–2, Carmelite friary 112
Banffshire 5, sheriffdom 4
Bangor, castle 25, diocese 84, Dominican friary 107

Bannockburn 32
Bannow Bay 23
Bardney, Benedictine monastery 86
Bardolf, Lord 42
Bardsey, Austin monastery 98
Barham, Crutched Friars 114
Barlynch, Austin monastery 98
Barnard Castle, Austin friary 110
Barnet, battle of 54
Barnstable, Cluniac monastery 95
Barnstaple, mint 16, 58–9
Barnwell, Austin monastery 98
Baron's Revolt 26
Barrow Gurney, Benedictine nunnery 88
Barton, Austin monastery 98
Basedale, Cistercian nunnery 92
Basingwen, Cistercian monastery 90
Basingwerk, castle 25
Bassishaw Ward, London 69
Bastides 27
Bath 12, 78, 121, Benedictine monastery 86, cloth production 73, diocese 81–2, mint 16, 58–9
Battisford, Hospitaller house 115
Battle 86, Benedictine monastery 86
Baxterwood, Austin monastery 98
Bayham, Premonstratensian monastery 101
Beauchief, Premonstratensian monastery 101
Beaulieu, Benedictine monastery 86, Cistercian monastery 91
Beaumaris, castle 27, 48
Beauvale, Carthusian monastery 96
Bec-Hellouin, Benedictine monastery 87
Becket, Thomas, Archbishop of Canterbury 96
Bective, Cistercian nunnery 94
Beddgelert, Austin monastery 98
Bedford 26, Franciscan friary 104, mint 16, 58–9, 61
Bedfordshire 3
Bedwyn, mint 16, 58
Beeston, Austin monastery 98
Beeston, castle 48
Belvoir 26, Benedictine monastery 86m castle 48
Bemaccan, Franciscan friary 104
Benedictine Rule 86, 90, 103
Berden, Austin monastery 98
Berengaria 51
Bergen, Norway 52